Cool, Calm Parent

Cool, Calm Parent

How not to lose it with your kids

Hollie Smith

Editor Roni Jay

Viva Books
New Delhi | Mumbai | Chennai | Kolkata
Bangalore | Hyderabad | Kochi | Guwahati

First Indian Edition 2010

VIVA BOOKS PRIVATE LIMITED

- 4737/23 Ansari Road, Daryaganj, New Delhi 110 002
  E-mail: vivadelhi@vivagroupindia.net, Tel. 42242200
- 76, Service Industries, Shirvane, Sector 1, Nerul, Navi Mumbai 400 706
  E-mail: vivamumbai@vivagroupindia.net, Tel. 27721273, 27721274
- Jamals Fazal Chambers, 26 Greams Road, Chennai 600 006
  E-mail: vivachennai@vivagroupindia.net, Tel. 28290304, 28294241
- B-103, Jindal Towers, 21/1A/3 Darga Road, Kolkata 700 017
  E-mail: vivakolkata@vivagroupindia.net, Tel. 22836381, 22816713
- 7, Sovereign Park Apartments, 56-58, K. R. Road, Basavanagudi, Bangalore 560 004
  E-mail: vivabangalore@vivagroupindia.net, Tel. 26607409, 26607410
- 101-102 Mughal Marc Apartments, 3-4-637 to 641, Narayanguda, Hyderabad 500 029
  E-mail: vivahyderabad@vivagroupindia.net, Tel. 27564481, 27564482
- Beevi Towers, First Floor, SRM Road, Kaloor, Kochi 682 018, Kerala
  E-mail: vivakochi@vivagroupindia.net, Tel: 0484-2403055, 2403056
- 232, GNB Road, Beside UCO Bank, Silpukhuri, Guwahati 781 003
  E-mail: vivaguwahati@vivagroupindia.net, Tel: 0361-2666386

www.vivagroupindia.com

Published by arrangement with

Crimson Publishing,
a division of Crimson Business Ltd
Westminster House, Kew Road
Richmond, Surrey TW9 2ND

ISBN : 978-81-309-1494-7

Published by Vinod Vasishtha for Viva Books Private Limited, 4737/23, Ansari Road, Daryaganj, New Delhi - 110 002.

Printed and bound by Raj Press, R-3, Inderpuri, New Delhi - 110 012.

Contents

Introduction

Anger – as any psychologist will tell you – can be a pretty destructive emotion. And unfortunately – as any parent will tell you – children are among the most anger-inducing human beings to inhabit the planet.

Maybe kids have always been annoying, and parents were always cross. But it does seem to be a particularly modern problem. Perhaps it's because mums and dads these days are stressed out, pushed for time, and overheated like never before; and our overindulged, overstimulated, media-junkie kids are more 'challenging' than their 'seen and not heard' predecessors. The weight of expectations doesn't help: sometimes it feels as if we're all competing in the lifestyle Olympics, striving to take the gold with our lovely homes, good jobs, and organically fed, over-achieving children. Some hope.

Personal experience was the main driving force for me in writing this book – it's a subject very close to my heart. As someone with a fairly short temper at the best of times, I've had my tolerance levels strained to the limit just about every single day since I had my first daughter, six years ago. I used to think I was so ill-tempered I should probably get some therapy and that I was, well, a very bad mother indeed. But then I started talking to my friends, and I realised it wasn't just me. In fact, a huge number of other parents admitted that they were frequently driven up the wall and beyond by their offspring.

I'll never forget a conversation I once had with my friend Julie, one of those enviable women who exudes an air of calm control in every aspect of her life, particularly when it comes to mothering her four-year-old son. Over coffee one day, while our kids played, I tentatively raised the subject of my dreadful temper and asked if she ever lost control with her little boy.

"God, yes," she said. "Only this morning I got so stressed out I told him to f***ing well put his clothes on, or else."

Having swapped dozens of similarly honest anecdotes now with other parents, I've established that I'm not *especially* abnormal, and I've stopped feeling guilty about my anger issues. But I haven't stopped wanting to challenge them.

You don't have to be a psychologist to understand that parental anger is not a particularly useful weapon in the battleground of domestic life. Losing your rag won't win you respect or gain you control, and neither is it setting the right example or smoothing the path for a good relationship with your child in the long term. It's such a waste, too. 'Quality time' may be a bit of a cliché, but there's no denying it's at a premium for modern families, and it's a great shame to fritter any of it away on confrontations. There's our emotional and physical health to consider, too. A cool, calm parent is less likely to be stressed, ill, sleepless, frustrated and resentful. And it follows that their children will be happier and healthier, too.

Accepted wisdom has it that it's the kids with the behavioural issues, not the adults. But maybe we need to acknowledge that's not always the case. After all, it's not necessarily the kids who are throwing the wobblers, sulking and barking petty insults. Sometimes it's the grown-ups, too. That's why you won't find any advice in here on ways to tackle your child's behaviour – there are loads of books on that subject already. What it *is* about is our responses to their behaviour. In short, it's a guide to anger management, for mums and dads.

So, just how *do* you become a cool, calm parent? (An oxymoron, surely!) I can't claim to have a magic bullet here. If only I did – by this time next year, I'd be a miwl'yunaire. And this book is definitely *not* about trying to banish anger, stress and frustration entirely – indeed, it would be a foolhardy tome if that was its intention. But it *is* about doing everything you can to be less angry, less often – for your own sake, as much as for your children's. It's about how you can cope with anger when it *does* rear its head, so that you let rip in constructive rather than destructive ways, and about damage limitation, once things have already gone pear-shaped.

There are also some useful thoughts on how to live a cooler, calmer lifestyle in general, which will hopefully make those family flashpoints fewer and further between.

I've consulted and referred to a number of experts to get a professional take on the matter. And, perhaps even more importantly, I've also cajoled a broad range of real parents into sharing their experiences and advice.

My aim here is not to add to anyone's guilt, or to raise the stakes a notch for those striving, pointlessly, to be 'perfect parents'. We're all in the same boat and, frankly, as captain of the good ship Lose-it, I am in no position to lecture. But there's a whole load of reassuring advice and useful tips here for anyone who'd like to be a cooler, calmer parent than they are right now. I can personally testify that the strategies in this book are helpful. I use them myself, every day of my life.

And if nothing else, you'll realise it's not just you. Kids can make you cross. It's a fact of life.

An important note

We're assuming that people reading this book – ill-tempered and stressed-out though they may be – are not affected by issues such as violence, abuse, addiction, or mental health problems: if you are, you will need more significant help than we can offer here. Some appropriate contact details are listed on the White Ladder Press website.

Acknowledgements

My heartfelt thanks to all the experts who kindly advised on the clever bits, in particular to the unfailingly helpful Dr Angharad Rudkin. Thanks to my other half Andy, provider of emotional and actual sustenance – and a far cooler, calmer, parent than I am; to my own mum, Tricia Smith, without whose support I would probably never have written it in the first place. And, of course, to my daughters Lily and Isabel, who so thoughtfully provide me with many opportunities to work on my cool, calm parenting skills.

1

Why your kids make you cross – and why that's OK

I never even knew I had a temper until I had children. It was very frightening that these children I loved so much, for whom I had sacrificed so much, could arouse such intense feelings of rage in me, their mother, whose primary responsibility was to nurture and protect them.
Nancy Samalin, from *Love and Anger: the Parental Dilemma* (Penguin, 1991)

It's a mad, mad world

We're all getting increasingly stressed, less calm, and more angry – there doesn't seem much doubt about that. You only have to take a look in the papers to know we're all suffering from road rage, air rage and even trolley rage. And perhaps it's no surprise, for even though in many ways we have it easy these days, the fact is that modern life is a lot like a motorway – everyone's going too fast.

As for parents, well, we're one of the most collectively stressed and irritable groups of people around. No one's coined a term for it yet – let's be original, and call it kid rage.

Why should this be so? After all, we're a lot more fortunate than previous generations of mothers and fathers – wealthier, healthier, and with technology on our side to ease the burden: blenders to make the baby food, washing machines to get the PE kit clean, websites to turn to for parenting advice, and on-tap television to serve as babysitter when we're too tired to take any more.

The downside is that we face a great many more pressures and have less time in which to tackle them. Mums as well as dads are working hard in demanding jobs, which means there are fewer hours in the day in which to relax and enjoy the good things about family life. And the pressure to do, have and be, is huge – for children, as well as for grown-ups. Materialism is the norm, and that helpful thing called technology has upped the pace – we want things, and we want things fast. It all adds up to ever-increasing stress levels. And stress makes us more prone to anger and less able to cope with life's little challenges – our kids among them.

Dr Angharad Rudkin, a child clinical psychologist who specialises in anger management, agrees that in many ways the stakes are higher for modern parents. "I think there's an overload of roles," she says. "In the 'good old days', Dad went off to work, Mum had tea on the table when he came back, and the kids were seen and not heard. I'm not saying this was a happy state of affairs, but at least people knew what their roles were.

"Nowadays, women have to be yummy mummies, career women, party organisers, trophy wives. Dads have to be family men as well as breadwinners, bathing the kids on their return from work, and taking them to exciting places on their days off. Add in the pressures of driving miles to school (far further than the local one, but preferable because of its Ofsted results); SATS exams for children as young as ten, and having to have three holidays a year just like the other families you know ... something has got to give. And that tends to be tempers."

Parenting, as few of us need telling, is a tough job. It's unwaged, you rarely get time off, and even though you're supposed to be the boss, no one ever seems to do what you tell them. It's hardly surprising if the strain shows sometimes.

You're not crazy. You're normal

Just to get this straight from the start: it is absolutely and fundamentally normal for parents to lose their cool, blow their top and get steamed up because of their children. For one thing, anger is a perfectly natural human response. And for another – for reasons that are explored below – no one can light the touch papers of temper quite like the under-age person or people sharing your home and answering to the title 'son' or 'daughter'. Which is why your average family home can sometimes be more war zone than comfort zone.

If you need further reassurance, here's what US parenting guru Nancy Samalin, author of *Love and Anger: The Parental Dilemma (Penguin, 1991)* has to say on the matter: "All parents experience anger, some more than others. We love our children to death, but the other side of the coin is feeling great anger and rage and guilt. I think it has to do with the fact that we're so invested in them. Another thing that I think contributes is the feeling of helplessness our children give us. You think of yourself as a competent person – if you ask another adult to do something for you, they usually do. Then you go home and ask your two-year-old to get in the bath and she looks at you and says no! It's very hard to feel loving towards a child who's having a knock-down tantrum. It makes us furious. But it's perfectly normal, and I think it's helpful and important for parents to realise that."

Why kids get our goat

Children have a large number of tendencies and characteristics that are annoying, purely by dint of the fact that they are children.

They can be careless, hasty, inquisitive, irrational, over-sensitive, hyper-emotional, whiny, demanding, obstinate, dramatically affected by practical factors such as fatigue or hunger, given to procrastination, and just plain daft.

These are merely drawbacks – along with the huge increase in food bills and laundry, and the annihilation of your social life – that you have to accept when you decide to have a family. (Fortunately, kids also come with a whole load of other, more loveable qualities, which balance their more 'challenging' traits. And also, being the fruit of our loins, we tend to instinctively forgive them these things, anyway.)

However, there is also a number of rather more deep-seated reasons why parents are driven potty by their offspring.

ONE: We love 'em ... so sometimes we hate 'em, too

From the moment they're first placed in our arms, our children trigger huge depths of feeling and huge emotional responses – love (all being well) is the first and foremost. But it's a package deal – get one emotion, you get them all.

"Parenting is a hugely intense experience which requires investment hour after hour, year after year," points out Dr Angharad Rudkin. "With such a 24/7 task, you're going to feel the whole gamut of emotions very intensely. Because we feel that we are entirely responsible for this little thing, we'll be pressuring ourselves on a daily basis to 'do it right', and when things don't go according to plan, as they often don't in families, it can feel like a big deal."

TWO: They are soooo immature

Children, adolescents and even later teens can't really be expected to have developed the full range of thinking, social, moral and behavioural skills that we adults have, including the ever-useful ability to rationalise and, also, to predict consequences. They don't always think things through and have a tendency to live for the moment, rather than swiftly calculating what the implications of their actions might be.

So, whilst your average 39-year-old woman, for example, knows full well that she must pack away the day's detritus come bedtime, because otherwise it will be yet another thing on tomorrow's to-do list, your average eight-year-old won't go through the same thought process. Or he might, but he won't draw the same, sensible conclusion. Not because he's a selfish, uncaring degenerate whose raison d'etre is to make life hard work for you. But because he's a kid.

(The age at which they should legitimately be expected to be in possession of all these wonderful skills is debatable. When you think about it, an awful lot of us grown-ups have yet to acquire the full complement ourselves.)

THREE: They're programmed to push their luck

Kids of all ages instinctively tend to nudge and nibble at what they know to be boundaries as a way of asserting their own burgeoning independence, and also, although it may seem ironic, as a way of testing our love for them. So, the next time your 18-month-old pushes her bowl of freshly prepared dinner to the floor for the fifth time in ten minutes, you could try reminding yourself that she's *not* merely being an infuriating little toe-rag who derives a sadistic pleasure from seeing you on your knees, simultaneously weeping and wiping the floor. She is merely asserting her independence and testing your love. Bless!

FOUR: They're desperate for our attention

Children want to be loved, cherished and accepted, just as adults want to be loved, cherished and accepted. We grown-ups are rational and secure enough to recognise when we've got all those things and, also, we've developed an ability to support ourselves, regardless. But children are not so sure, and they are constantly craving signs that they're loved and accepted through attention – particularly from their parents, who they want to love and accept them most of all. Unfortunately, they will take attention in any way they can get it – good, bad, or ugly. Which, inevitably, can strain our patience to the limit.

Why anger can be a good thing

Anger is a perfectly normal emotion, just like any other, including happiness, sadness, guilt and jealousy. We're wired to get heated when we feel under threat or frustrated; in fact, it's a survival function – if we didn't feel angry about difficult situations, we wouldn't be stirred into resolving them. It also provides 'decompression', allowing us, in theory, to release strong feelings rather than store them up, unhealthily, inside.

What's more, a certain amount of fury in families is no bad thing: if expressed in the right way, anger can actually be a *positive* step towards resolving conflicts and problems, and communicating the way we feel. And sometimes we *do* need to release all that angers, annoys and generally frustrates us, because holding on to too much of it, for too long, may not be very good for us, both psychologically and physically (as the list of potential health problems listed below indicates).

Besides all that, kids need to know that anger and conflict are normal things, that they shouldn't be held in or brushed aside, and that there are ways and means of resolving them and getting over it. Kids also need to be encouraged – terrifying though this may sound – to find healthy ways of expressing their own anger, so it's not necessarily a bad thing for them to see their parents do so.

As Nancy Samalin puts it: "Anger is a very basic emotion, a part of who we are, and it's got to go somewhere. You can't keep sitting on it."

A health warning

Having said all that, neither is it particularly good for us (or the poor beggars in the firing line) to express our anger to excess, releasing it willy-nilly whenever we're perturbed in the form of physical or verbal aggression. This sort of behaviour can be hurtful and destructive, as well as a pretty poor example to be setting kids. And too much of the 'exploding' sort of emotions can also take their toll on our health.

Whether you tend to bury it deep down (these people are sometimes called 'imploders'), or whether you tend to let it rip (and these people are sometimes called – you guessed it – 'exploders'), it's widely believed that excessive or long-term anger and stress may be risk factors in a range of physical conditions. These include:

- High blood pressure (hypertension)
- Heart disease and stroke
- Gastric ulcers
- Raised cholesterol levels
- Bowel conditions such as IBS or colitis
- Headaches, migraines and sinus problems
- Back strain
- Insomnia
- Increased susceptibility to infection
- Skin disorders
- Some cancers

And then of course, there are the psychological and emotional issues that they are linked to, including:

- Depression
- Guilt
- Lack of self-esteem and self-confidence

> Whenever you find yourself on the verge of losing your cool, ask yourself this question: is this worth raising my blood pressure, wearing out my cardiovascular system, and eventually causing a heart attack?
> **W. Doyle Gentry, from *Anger Management for Dummies* (Wiley Publishing, 2007)**

Why are some of us more angry than others?

We all get angry at some time or another, but some of us a lot more often, and to a far greater extent, than others. That's because we're all working against different backdrops. Some of us may have more stressful factors working against us in life. And, of course, some of us deal better with those factors than others, anyway, according to our temperaments and personalities.

How we arrived at those temperaments and personalities probably involved a complex journey. If one or both of our parents were irascible sorts, that will more than likely be relevant. They may well have passed on the trait, although whether through the genes they've given us (ie by 'nature') or the example they set and attitudes they have (ie by 'nurture') is a debate that rumbles on. Most people agree these days that it's unlikely to be one or the other, but some combination of the two.

Knowing that your short fuse was inherited is no excuse, though. If bad tempers are passed on like red hair, or a passion for football, then that's a very good reason to keep check on it when your own kids are around. Those of us with irascible natures simply have to work harder than others to keep the worst of our tempers contained. It's our chance to break the pattern.

As Angharad Rudkin explains: "We're all born with certain predispositions – whether that's to having a loud voice, running quickly, or getting angry. This predisposition does not guarantee that you will develop that thing (you never know, I may have a predisposition to be brilliant at running backwards up hills but because I have never been in an environment where I've had to try that, it remains a predisposition only.) So, we could be born with a short fuse but if we have really strong models of adults dealing with frustration in positive ways, we're less likely to build on that predisposition. In other words, you may be born with it, and even be brought up with it, but it doesn't guarantee you are going to end up being it."

> Our early experiences of how others deal with anger and how our expressions of anger have been responded to will have a significant effect on how we respond to our own and others' anger ...
> **Adrian Faupel, Elizabeth Herrick and Peter Sharp, from *Anger Management: A Practical Guide* (1998, David Fulton)**

> *If you suspect that an angry parent has had a very negative or long-term impact on you, and the way you deal with your own family, you may benefit from some counselling. You could try Relate (which isn't just for couples, it's for people experiencing emotional difficulties in any sort of relationship), go to your GP (although there will usually be a long wait for counselling on the NHS), or check out private counselling and psychotherapy practitioners in your area. Look in the telephone book or online at one of the following: the British Association for Counselling and Psychotherapy's UK Register of Counsellors, the UK Council for Psychotherapy, or the British Psychological Society. Website and other contact details are listed on the White Ladder Press website.*

Do unto others

All of which is a bit confusing – is it OK to be angry with your kids and show them and tell them so, or not?

Well, children are fairly forgiving, resilient little folk, it's true – as a parent, you can get away with a certain amount of OTT ranting without them hating you as a result, or growing up emotionally damaged. Which is just as well, because they'd grow up with a pretty misleading view of the world if they didn't see anyone lose their rag once in a while. And sometimes, it's no bad thing for kids to see that their more 'challenging' behaviour has consequences of the unpleasant variety – ie that it makes someone feel angry and makes them do angry things like shout.

But for the most part, it's better all round if we can find what the experts variously call 'healthy', 'positive', or 'effective' ways of relieving and expressing all the anger, frustration and stress that's part and parcel of parenting.

Why? Well, clearly, those of us who love our children (and I'm assuming that anyone who'll bother to pick up this book certainly does) will not want to hurt, worry or intimidate them with extreme reactions or excessive behaviour. And from an adult perspective, it almost always feels crap when you've said or done something to your children you wish you hadn't.

"It's scary for a child when their parent screams at them. And yes, you can control children with fear but it's not a good thing for them to be experiencing. They don't have the strategies to cope with it, as adults do, and it could have implications for their emotional health," says Annette Mountford, chief executive of Family Links, an organisation dedicated to helping parents have happy relationships with their children [*www.familylinks.org.uk*]. "As a parent you feel awful, too, after a major loss of temper. And that's bad for *your* emotional health."

Of course, there's also that unavoidable business of setting a good example. There's no way round it, really, it's down to us to teach our children how best to behave in this world, by 'modelling' the behaviour we hope of them. And you don't need a degree in psychology to work out that parents who go around losing their cool at the drop of a hat are likely to end up with kids who do so, too.

"Children learn what their parents *do* as well as say," says Dr Angharad Rudkin. "Whatever happens at home, children are going to think that's the norm. So if that involves lots of arguing, shouting or major sulks, then chances are that's the way the child is going to express their own feelings, inside and outside the home."

So, it's not really *whether* you get angry with your kids (because of course, it's a rare parent who doesn't), but how you express it and how you cope with it that counts.

And how best to cope when your children make you cross? Well, that's what the rest of the book's about. So please, do read on ...

> Conflict is inherent in all families simply because its members have different interests, personalities, temperaments, values, wants, likes, dislikes, anxieties – all of which have to be negotiated if the family is to operate in relative harmony. The major distinction between healthy and unhealthy families is how they choose to resolve these conflicts – not whether they have conflicts in the first place.
> **W. Doyle Gentry, from *Anger Management for Dummies* (Wiley Publishing Inc, 2007)**

PARENTS' PANEL: What do your kids do that really gets your goat?

Getting dressed is a flashpoint for us. I'll offer him two or three choices and he'll frequently say: "Don't *want* that one," often

throwing it across the room. He'll ask for something he knows is in the wash and whinge when he can't have it. Then he'll start reading a book or playing with a toy. Eventually after about ten minutes he selects an item and tries to put it on himself – if he doesn't get distracted by something else first. Sometimes he manages on his own but if he can't and I try to help he'll say, "No, *me* do it," and then get frustrated because he can't. Then, if his dad is doing something else, especially if it's holding his little brother, he'll say "Daddy do it," and push me away. Sometimes it takes half an hour to get dressed. If I'm really fed up, I say: "Well, go to nursery with no clothes on. I don't care!" and walk out the room. It drives me bananas.
Judy, mum to sons aged three and one

Whining and whinging – it drives me mad. They ask for something, I say I'll do it in a minute but they keep going on and on and on ... until I am so fed up I end up telling them that no, they are not getting whatever it was at all now.
Sharron, mum to kids aged six, three and three months

At the moment, it's the arguing between two or three of them. It's usually over a toy, or the eldest will disagree with the youngest just to be obstreperous – and as he's just really starting to talk now, he can answer back. Then it escalates because they will keep on and on in the vein of "You did", "I didn't" etc. Also, they 'tell' on each other a lot.
Elizabeth, mum to kids aged seven, four and two

Sometimes he gets into a 'no' vibe and says 'no' to everything. He ends up sounding like Kevin the teenager. Do you want to go to the park? I don't want to. How about a treat? I don't want to.
Paul, dad to a son aged two

It's their untidiness and laziness that gets to me. Why do children, especially pre-teens, find it so difficult to put their dirty clothes into a laundry basket, which is placed opposite their bedroom door? Why do they leave their clothes hanging over the back of a chair, when they've only worn them for two hours? And why don't they ever flush the loo when they have had a poo? I appreciate that they understand about not wasting water, but this is taking saving the planet too far.

These circumstances are continual. No matter how many times I've explained that they should not do these things, they still do them.

Recently I'd spent all day cleaning the house until I was dead on my feet – we were expecting visitors – only to discover that the kids had come in from outside, gone in to the kitchen and helped themselves to squash and chocolate spread sandwiches leaving a trail of finger marks all over the worktops, doors and walls, and breadcrumbs all up the stairs. They'd pulled toys out of cupboards, and to add insult to injury, one of them had had a poo in the downstairs loo and had not flushed the chain. My eldest was lying on the sofa, watching a DVD, eating a sandwich, and talking on the phone at the same time ... which is probably what sent me over the edge. I just lost it. I'm sure the neighbours all heard me. I really screamed at them: how dare they expect me to pick up after them? They were lazy, selfish children. Why can they never clean up their own mess? How come there are five human beings living in this house, but only one of them does all the work? I was just so tired of cleaning and being taken for granted that I cracked.
Christine, mum to kids aged 13, 10, and nine

Untidiness. Nothing gets put away, lids don't get replaced and although they accept what I ask, when it comes to it, they simply don't remember.
Nick, dad to kids aged 17 and 10

A regular flashpoint for us is arriving home from school, and them breaking out into petty bickering and fighting, me having to remind them and yell at them to put bags away and get changed, and having to referee and keep them in separate areas of the house whilst they do this.
Lucy, mum to sons aged 10 and seven

He often completely ignores me when I am asking him not to do things. Or he says, "It's all right Mummy." Usually it's bouncing on furniture – especially at other people's houses. Oh, and wiping his nose with his hand and then putting his hand in his mouth and making horrible noises at the dinner table – both of which he's learnt at nursery.
Claire, mum to a son aged three

My daughter will *always* interrupt when being told off. And even if I'm not already cross I can almost physically feel my blood temperature rise. She won't listen. And when she hasn't anything constructive to say, she'll just make a noise. Have you ever tried to tell off someone who just won't let you speak? It's a very effective tactic, unfortunately.
Emma, mum to kids aged 17 and 14

With my eldest, I suppose it's his lack of 'thinking'. And it's a vicious circle – he's used to me doing everything for him, so he has no need to do much or remember stuff for himself and yet I do it, because he can't remember anything. I pack his bag for school, go through his timetable, repeating myself non-stop, in the hope that some of it will go in. My in-laws and my hubby laugh at his ways (apparently my hubby was much the same) but I fail to see the funny side of it, as an organised person myself. I find his lack of motivation hard to accept.

As for my youngest, dinner is still a flashpoint – too much talking, and slow eating. He's always the first to sit down and the

last to eat. And he can never finish his dinner because he's ' full up', yet an hour later claims he's hungry. He's very confident, too, and sometimes I would like a little less 'backchat' from him.
Rosie, mum to sons aged 11 and 5

Repeatedly asking for things you've already said 'no' to, or going to ask their dad when I've already said said 'no' – that's spine-ticklingly infuriating.
Fiona, mum to kids aged six and four

Trigger points for me tend to be constant demands: my three-year-old is incessantly in the kitchen asking for a drink, snack, banana, raisins, etc. He opens the fridge door and peers in to see what he can have next – it drives me mad. I've sworn at him, I'm afraid, and he did repeat it (only to his dad, thank God). "It's a f***ing blueberry" was the phrase. Eeek, ouch – nightmare, I know. Other 'flashpoints' are my seven-year-old son winding up the three-year-old. The teasing and taunting drives me insane – the three-year-old has a very loud whine which then wakes up the baby and they all end up in tears. The seven-year-old then says I don't love him any more and that I wish he'd never been born. Arrrrgh!
Antonia, mum to kids aged seven, three and eight months

I get angry with the children when I feel like I'm being fobbed off. For example, I'll ask the boys why they have stuffed countless empty sweet wrappers under the sofa, and their answer will be, "I'm not sure," or "It wasn't me." This will usually result in me ranting at them and cause my wife to come in and speak calmly until I sink back into the trance of cooking and cleaning up after everyone.

Conversely, my wife will lose her rag with the eldest for not tidying her room after several requests to do so. Usually it's my turn

to speak calm words to her at that point.
Nick, dad to daughters aged 16, 14, and 5, and twin boys of 11

Every weekend the kids try everything within their power to anger me. This can include making the biggest mess, grinding food into just cleaned carpets, asking for the world in the space of a second, bickering with each other, making a loud screech (which my daughter does very well and which seems to go through your bones), getting each other in trouble, putting loo roll down the toilet (a whole loo roll, may I add), washing their hands in the bathroom and making sure everywhere has soap attached to it, and eating half their lunch before deciding they don't want it any more. Now I know most kids do this but there is a limit that one person can take and my kids do it all and more in the space of a few hours. I work full-time and try to make sure my time with the children is quality as I don't have the option of quantity. But I swear they know that I have two days off a week and that it's wind-up Mummy time.
Vicki, mum to kids aged four and two

Our three-year-old son is waging a war of attrition at the moment. It's like guerilla warfare against a superior force who he knows ultimately he can't beat, but he keeps landing annoying small victories along the way anyway. One of us will be getting him dressed or giving him his Cheerios, when halfway through he'll demand the other one does it – the old "mummy/daddy do it" routine, which drives us mad as he plays off one against the other.
Adrian, dad to sons aged three and one

I seem to lose my rag with her nearly every day at the moment. Let's take yesterday, for example. I'm asking her to "come here". By name. So no excuse for not knowing it is her I am talking to. OK, so perhaps the fact that she is only 21 months old is a fair excuse, but I wasn't having that one yesterday. She's three feet

away and after calling her about six times she hasn't even turned round to look at me, so I grab her by her nappy and drag her towards me and turn her to face me. I tell her that she *must* listen when Mummy is talking to her. Of course I then remembered the bit about her only being 21 months old and I end up feeling like the meanest bully on the block.
Karen, mum to a daughter aged 21 months and a son aged six months

ANGER MANAGEMENT: top tips from experts

Number one: The Traffic Lights Technique

- Think of **Red**: Stop, recognise your anger
- Think of **Amber**: Start to think calmly about the way forward
- Think of **Green**: Once your anger's subsided, calmly move forward.

William Davies, from *Overcoming Anger and Irritability* (Constable and Robinson, 2000)

2

Tiptoeing round trouble

> When I was first starting out as an idealistic young clinical psychology student, things seemed so much clearer and easier. I'd sit in rooms with tired, desperate parents and wonder how they couldn't see the problem. "The secret," I would tell those poor people, "is that you have to be consistent." Somewhere along the way I had children of my own, and then everything changed. Now my definition of consistency is that if I can consistently avoid the all-too-frequent urge to throw the kids out the window, it's a good day.
>
> **Nigel Latta, from *Before Your Kids Drive You Crazy, Read This!* (HarperCollins, 2006)**

Know your flashpoints

Now, this may well be a case of stating the bleedin' obvious, but the first step towards becoming a cooler, calmer parent is to try and avoid the situations that make you cross in the first place.

Being one step ahead of trouble is a skill that requires quick-thinking and a certain amount of perception, and it generally takes a fair bit of parenting experience to hone. But boy, is it useful – if you can pre-empt stressful situations or moments of conflict altogether, whenever possible, you automatically save yourself bother before it actually arises.

Flashpoints – those issues and events that precipitate trouble – often repeat themselves, so it's worth establishing any that come up over and over in your house, and tiptoeing round them for all you are worth. Don't feel this is in any way a cop-out, or simple overindulgence of the little blighters. It's just taking sensible precautions.

If there are troublespots that arise repeatedly in your home, take a while to identify them (jot them down if it helps), and have a think about what you can do to avoid them in the future – or better still, to remove them from the agenda entirely. There's often a very simple solution – it just may not have actually occurred to you.

Here's an example: we used to have a bit of an issue with these two pink plastic cereal bowls in our house. One of them had a mermaid design on it, the other a fairy. But both my girls had a preference for the fairy. Finally exhausted by the whole "it's my turn to have the fairy" routine and the levels of fury it invoked in me, I very quietly secreted the bowls in the back of the cupboard – where they still languish unused – and introduced identical plain white china ones, muttering something about how grown up they were now, by way of distraction.

To this day, I always go to considerable pains to hunt out exactly the same type of bowl (and spoon – we have cutlery issues, too) for each of my girls at breakfast every morning. I also measure out equal quantities of cereal, milk and sugar to quite anally retentive degrees, which bypasses the whole heated "she's got more than me" debate.

Some people may consider this makes me a bit of a sap. Well, I don't care. I know from experience that these matters are very commonly flashpoints in our house, and what's more, the mornings are always very fraught generally so the last thing I need is a squabble over something I can easily avoid.

We've all been there

Recognise any of these common flashpoints? (I don't have the solutions. Just thought it might make you feel better to know they're universal)

School mornings *They've been getting dressed for half an hour and they're still not beyond the vest and pants stage. They secreted their school bag somewhere the previous evening and its whereabouts is apparently classified information. They won't stay still while you attempt to coax their hair into a lice-bustingly tight French plait. They tell you just as you're about to leave that they need the ingredients for a Victoria sandwich cake / a costume for the play they're in that afternoon / a home-baked loaf for the Harvest Festival.*

Bedtimes *They won't go to bed. They won't go to sleep. They reappear after you've settled them wanting "a drink" or "something to eat". They come into your room at night and want to get into your bed. They wake and yell at you to come into their bedrooms.*

Mealtimes *They won't come to the table, however much you shout. They won't eat what you've spent ages preparing, or they chuck it around (forgivably or otherwise, depending on how old they are). They complain that they don't like something (even though they ate it a month ago). They're still eating two hours after they started. Their manners are atrocious.*

Conflict between siblings *They want to watch different television programmes. One of them has hold of the thing the other one desires. The youngest has hit the oldest – no reason, he just has. They're bickering about something so utterly unimportant it makes you want to scream.*

Rudeness, whinging, wittering, selective deafness *They make loud, impolite demands without so much as a please or thank* *you. You've shouted up the stairs for them to come down 48 times – and they still haven't. They keep asking for something even if you've said no ... and asking, and asking. They've just told you to piss off – and they're only five. They won't answer your questions. They won't stop asking you questions.*

Mess and destruction *They've left their bedroom looking like a bomb's hit it. All the bedrooms, in fact. And the sitting room. And the dining room. And the garden. They've left all their drawers open – so far out, the chest is in danger of toppling over. The consequences of their five-minute art session is around half an hour's clearing up for you. What started as a wholesome and bonding cookie-bake has ended in devastation – actual and emotional.*

Matters sartorial *They won't get dressed (see above). It's sub-zero outside and they won't wear their coat. Or hat. Or gloves. Or scarf. They won't put their shoes on. They won't wear the clothes you buy them. They will only wear the clothes you hate.*

Don't forget the kids' flashpoints too. If you recognise them you can head off trouble that you know will wind you up. If you always get stressed by those four words every parent hates – "I need a pee" – when you're half-way round the supermarket, make sure you visit the loo first before you put anything in the trolley. I know it won't always work, but it should keep your blood pressure down more often than not.

Likewise, if you have one of those children who gets grouchy and bad tempered when they're hungry, recognising that this is a moment to shove a banana or a quick sandwich at them can save you from the outburst (yours, not theirs) that they're bound to instigate otherwise.

Make life easy on yourself (aka cut yourself some slack, or lower your standards)

Do you sometimes make life more stressful than it actually needs to be by demanding too much of your kids, and of yourself? Modern parents are very much prey to this, sadly. We're in a state of constant anxiety about whether we're doing the right thing by our children and when we feel we're failing, the unsurprising result is that we're stressed out and over-emotional about it.

You can make life far less of a struggle if you work out which things really matter and are therefore worth fighting for – naturally, different people will have different ideas about what these are. On everything else, cut yourself (and your kids) some slack.

Sometimes the key to reducing stress and eliminating flashpoints is a simple acknowledgement that whatever it is that's bothering you *really doesn't have to.* I used to get cross, for example, with my younger one, because she insisted on making the sartorial choices of an insane old lady. Then I realised that, since she is three, it doesn't actually *matter* what she's wearing (as long as she's wearing something). Now I let her make her own mind up. Well, at least she's individual.

If the basics are in place (do your kids eat enough to keep them alive? Are they reasonably kind to animals and smaller children? Do they know that you love them? Again, these things are probably subjective), then you don't have to let the rest of it be a cause for conflict.

> If your buttons are being pushed, it's important for you to look at the standards you hold. Your standards may be hard or even impossible to live up to ... when parents raise the bar too high, everyone loses.
>
> **Bonnie Harris, from *When Your Kids Push Your Buttons* (Warner Books Inc, 2003)**

Letting the little things Go (aka pick your battles, or, don't sweat the small stuff)

You can extend the whole 'Make Life Easy on Yourself' approach beyond a general philosophy – it's helpful for dealing with specific incidents, too. A cliché it may be, but it makes a lot of sense to 'Let the Little Things Go'.

Commonly in family life, situations can seem much worse than they actually are. Psychologists have some fancy words for this kind of tendency – they call it 'catastrophising', or 'awfulising', and it basically means blowing a situation out of all proportion.

If you can satisfy yourself that a situation is really *not* worth the hassle, you should. Always take a moment to assess the matter at hand and ask: is this as bad as I think it is? Sure, if your youngest has just attacked your eldest with a blunt instrument or something of a similar scale, you need to wade in with strong disapproval and the appropriate consequences. But very often, you'll find the answer is "no". In which case, you may well decide it's not worth pushing your pulse soaring.

It can really help to stop and call in some perspective. Be flexible, wherever possible. And run through a quick mental checklist before you jump in with a negative reaction: does the matter at hand actually matter? Is what they've just done truly naughty – or is it just something they've done because they're irrational, immature, clumsy or just not actually all that clever yet (in other words, because they're a kid)? If they've put in a request and, without thinking, your immediate inclination is to say '"no", do you actually have a good reason for your refusal? (Though of course, if you have, you should stand firm.)

I'm not suggesting for a minute you let your kids rule the roost, or get away with anything dangerous, disrespectful, or downright wrong just for an easy life. Rules, routines and boundaries are important props for family life – otherwise chaos would reign. Just that there's usually a fair bit of scope to relax over stuff which, given a moment's thought, may not be as bad as you think.

"The more of this you can do the better. I always tell parents to ask themselves, how important is this, and will it matter a week from now?" says Nancy Samalin, author of *Love and Anger: The Parental Dilemma (Penguin, 1991)*. "Let's assume your child is going to school in clashing clothes or wearing party shoes instead of sneakers. It's not going to matter that much. If they have cookies for lunch instead of something nutritious, big deal. Say to yourself, what's the worst thing that can happen if I don't make a fuss about it? Have negotiable and non-negotiable rules. If the thing at hand is on the first of those lists, then maybe you can let it slide."

Sue Atkins, parenting coach and author of *Parenting for Dummies (Wiley and Sons, 2007)*, agrees that you need to work out what's important and what isn't. "Letting it go will mean different things to different people – some parents are control freaks and others have no boundaries at all. As a general rule of thumb, you've got to have boundaries in place, but if you find yours are making you stressed and winding you up, something's not right and it's time to look at them. You do need to work out the framework of your values, though, first," she says.

So, it's a good idea to establish the things that really matter to you. You may well feel strongly about clean rooms, good table manners, rigid bedtimes, strict limits for screen time, co-ordinated garments, or a total ban on artificial additives. And if you do, fair enough: everyone's entitled to have things that really matter to them. On the other hand, you may decide to file them (or whatever else is relevant to you personally) under 'negotiable' – then you know that when you smell trouble you can give in before it even becomes an issue.

Often, it's tempting to let something go even if it's on your non-negotiable list. And that's OK, too, but you do need to bear in mind that children have elephant-like powers of recall in these matters – they won't let you forget that you let them get away with it once before. So, when you're weighing up a situation and considering leniency, keep in mind that you are setting a precedent. If it's something you know is going to cause you grief in the future, you may be better off standing firm. At the very least, you'll need to make clear that it's a special offer, perhaps by creating a spurious excuse for the let-off. For instance, "I'm going to let you stay up and watch this programme but it's just this once, and only because I need to make an important phone call" (which you'll probably then have to disappear to pretend to be making).

Timing is also important. If you're going to give in, far better to do so at the beginning than standing firm for a while and then giving up because you can't be bothered to. As dreary a concept as consistency is, it's true that it's fairly important in child-rearing, and once you've stated a case pretty firmly, you really need to stick with it if you want them to take you seriously next time. Which is precisely why you need to work out the framework of your values in advance.

It's taken me six and a half years, but I've pretty much worked out the framework of *my* values. I've reassessed countless causes of fuss and friction – messy bedrooms, odd outfits, uneaten dinners and that extra episode of Scooby-Doo, for example – and I've come to the conclusion that these things, in my book at least, are *not* worth losing my cool over. As a result, I lose my cool far less frequently.

Cold legs won't kill them

Child-rearing experts often recommended that you allow children to experience the 'natural consequences' of their bad behaviour rather than punish them. So – to take two classic examples – if they won't put their coat on when you tell them to, you let them go outside and get thoroughly chilly. And if they let their room get untidy, you simply tell them "I told you so" when they can't find the toy they're looking for.

It certainly makes a great philosophy for any parent seeking to avoid unpleasant confrontations with naughty children. Key to it is not caring much yourself what those consequences may be, so you have to be OK about them going out in Arctic conditions and getting blue legs, or about their rooms having that 'just ransacked by professional burglars' look. If you can relax enough to put these sort of things in your 'doesn't matter' list, then you too can master the fine parental art of allowing them to experience the natural consequences of their actions.

You've gotta laugh

Sometimes a funny side rears its head in a situation and if it does, you should grab the opportunity with both hands and laugh things off. Heartily.

> Our little girl knows she's not meant to put things in the fish tank. But certain items have gone in that we just had to laugh about. My husband's binoculars, my mobile phone, a toy steak, and a plastic goldfish – which really seemed to confuse the real fish.
> **Pippa, mum to a daughter aged two**
>
> Humour? Thank God for it. My youngest son has a fab sense of humour, he'll probably be a comedian when he's older. I'll be all

> serious and be asking him to do something or trying to calm down, and he'll put on one of his voices and stroke my cheek, or something. So I end up laughing, his brothers are laughing, and that's that, all seriousness is out the window!
> **Lynne, mum to boys aged 22, 20 and 13**
>
> I was tired and stressed out after work and trying to give them a bath. My daughter was messing about and splashing me and her brother, despite me asking her not to, so I shouted at her to stop it. Then she lowered her eyes, looked at me and very deliberately splashed me and then giggled. So I splashed her back and then we had a water fight. Eventually we were all soaked, as was the bathroom.
> **Nina, mum to kids aged four and one**

Give yourself a break when you're at breaking point

Of course, sometimes your kids are only guilty of a minor offence anyway, but you're so stressed and tired that it doesn't seem possible that a boxful of spilt Frosties is anything but a complete and utter disaster.

Blow-outs often have little to do with the minor event that triggered them. They may be far more to do with how tired you are, what kind of day you've had or how you're feeling about yourself at that precise moment in time.

If you know you're not in a good mood for whatever reason, give yourself a break – literally. If you've got the luxury of a partner or some other reliable adult around, enlist their support and relinquish your duties. And if not, and someone's got to get the tea on the table or get the kids in the bath and into bed and that someone's got to be you, take whatever short cuts you can. Don't cook, give them sandwiches. Don't bath, let them go to bed grubby.

Don't fret about too much screen-time, let them watch more television.

In other words, sometimes you need to drop your standards to keep your temper intact and your stress levels normal. And that's a perfectly reasonable pay-off.

PARENTS' PANEL: Do you ever let things go for an easy life?

I'm not one of those mums who says "no" to everything. He can stick his hand down a drain, get as dirty as he likes, shove mud in his gob (he'll soon realise it doesn't taste that great), wear what he likes. And, because my boundaries are generally quite relaxed, when I do say no, I mean it.
Hannah, mum to a son aged 16 months

I once came in to find the kids had helped themselves to a giant bag of sweets whilst I was out in the garden and had eaten half of them. I was all ready to get mad, then I saw their guilty faces, thought, "Oh sod it, life's too short," and surprised them by saying they may as well finish them all.
Kelly, mum to kids aged six, four, and three

I very often do this. An example off the top of my head: I'll end up giving him chocolate spread sandwiches for breakfast with squash, instead of something healthy.
Bill, dad to a son aged three and twins aged 10 months

I believe you should choose your battles carefully otherwise you spend your whole time bickering and nagging. When he was two, I let him go to a posh wedding in his wellies, as he started to kick off as we got out of the car to go into the church. My mother-in-law wasn't impressed, but I'd rather have put up with her disapproval than the tantrum!
Jen, mum to boys aged three and nine months

I once was given some fantastic advice: "Don't sweat the small stuff'". I find this helps in lots of areas in my life. I'm quite an emotional person and I don't deal with stress easily, so I try to make my life as easy and peaceful as possible by just not getting into stressful situations in the first place. I let a lot of situations go because I think you could be forever picking them up on something and (a) what does that do for their self esteem? and (b) will they really listen to you, when you really need them to?
Rosie, mum to boys aged 11 and five

I always try to judge in advance if it is worth the hassle of intervening in a situation and sometimes let things pass. But I think that if you do say "stop" you have to follow it through.
Paul, dad to a son aged two

Frequently. For instance, normally I'd make them tidy up their mess but if they're tired after a long day, the fights and hassle I get isn't always worth it – it takes longer, we all end up frazzled, they go to bed in a mood, and I'm left feeling angry at them. It's far easier to let it slide that day and do it myself in 10 minutes flat.
Sharron, mum to daughters aged six, three, and six months

Sometimes we do give in for an easy life – and if we want to make it out of the door within the next hour.
Adrian, dad to boys aged three and one

I will sometimes choose to ignore or pretend not to see bad behaviour if I can't be bothered to deal with it, particularly if I am enjoying time chatting to a friend or something.
Charlotte, mum to kids aged four and two

I struggle with my daughter's dress sense. She wants to be hip and look fab, but I want her to be dressed sensibly for playschool, so that there will be no knickers showing when she

hangs upside down on the monkey bars, or her good clothes won't be destroyed by the grassy play area/paint/ink/ etc. I really struggle to buy her clothes that she will wear, and have to take her with me to choose her own things, then I end up spending a lot more that I planned. It infuriates me that she will not wear what I want her to wear, in my price range. But I let her get away with it anyway – just to keep the peace.
Angila, mum to kids aged six and two

Yep, for sure. I think it's about 'winning the war, not the battle' and so I'm a big believer in picking on the things that really matter, and letting other less important things slide – such as being cheeky, for example, or over-excitable. But I always pick up on manners.
Nina, mum to kids aged four and one

My missus hates the kids eating with their fingers. I don't mind, as long as they're eating.
Bob, dad to kids aged ten, four and two

ANGER MANAGEMENT: top tips from experts

Number two: The '*D*on't *G*et *T*oo *B*oiling' Technique

- **Distance** Once you feel your pace quickening, physically remove yourself from situation, either by taking a step backwards or walking away.
- **Ground** Bring yourself back to earth by distracting your brain from its emotive response to a situation with a mundane task such as counting all the 'blue' objects in a room; or mentally writing a shopping list.
- **Tension** Release tightly clenched muscles by clenching and unclenching fists or running up the stairs. Punch a cushion. Saying a phrase over and over such as 'calm' or 'cool' can be useful. Visualise a relaxing experience.

- **Breathe** Take three or four deep slow breaths. Try visualising the passage of your breath as it enters and leaves your body.

From *Managing Anger: Simple Steps to Dealing with Frustration and Threat*, by Gael Lindenfield (Thorsons, 2000)

3

Pause for thought

> It happens to every parent: one minute you're having a great time and feeling on top of the world. You're calm. You're patient. You're fun to be with. Then suddenly, without warning, you start to change. You feel your heart beating faster and your temper rising and suddenly you explode into the parent from Hell. Welcome to what I call a 'Parent Losing the Plot' moment.
> **Sue Atkins, from *Raising Happy Kids for Dummies* (Wiley, 2007)**

Hang on a moment

Well, Chapter 2 was all very well – *sometimes* you can avoid trouble, or at least pretend to be indifferent towards it. But of course, sometimes you can't, and there's no getting round the fact that you're about to lose your temper.

You can still pre-empt and rein in explosions by identifying those burgeoning emotions early on and acting to defuse them – in fact, psychotherapists and anger management experts labour the point that it's far easier to take control of your temper before you've *actually* lost it, and fury has swamped rational thought altogether.

> If I can see I'm about to lose my rag I sometimes fake it, when I still have the presence of mind. Obviously it would be better to

> stay calm but sometimes that's just not an option. The advantage is that it gets the scene over with before I've done or said anything I'll really regret, and I don't get that horrible feeling that goes with losing your temper.
> **Miranda, mum to sons aged 11 and five**

When you're angry, real time can go out the window, and it can feel as though you're on fast forward. Press the pause button – use an imaginary remote control, if it helps. Then take things in slow motion.

"When you're really angry, you can only see one line of thought," says counsellor Angela Rhydderch, who works extensively with parents and particularly in the field of anger management. "I often advise people to stop, and to look at the bigger picture, instead."

Try counting to 10, literally, before you speak or act – it will buy you some useful time to compose yourself. And if 10's not enough, try 20.

> When we stop there is the possibility for something different from rage to occur. By stopping we give ourselves time – time in which to determine the appropriate response to the situation and implement it. This rule of anger management makes sure you stop, step back and take time out before acting in the heat of the moment – and quite probably regretting it later.
> **Mike Fisher, from *Beating Anger* (Rider, 2005)**

What are your warning signs?

If you're going to cut angry outbursts before they've burst out, you need to be able to acknowledge the fact that you're getting angry. It's not always easy – sometimes tempers get lost so quickly it's hard to see them coming. But usually there'll be some warning signs.

We all tend to have a pattern to our anger cycles – what usually gets us there, what we usually do with it, and what we do to calm down again. All these things add up to our 'anger profile'.

It's helpful to be familiar with our own anger profile and in particular the early stages, which often include one or more fairly strong physical indications (some common ones are outlined below).

"The more you can get in touch with these physical symptoms of your anger, the more chance you will have to do something about it," says anger management counsellor Angela Rhydderch [*www.rhydderch.clara.net*].

In other words, once you know you're teetering on the brink, you've got valuable moments to work out how you're going to pull yourself back a little and avoid that downward plunge.

Stress signals: Signs that you're losing your cool

- heartbeat racing
- muscles tensing
- chest tightening
- stomach churning
- fists clenching
- body temperature rising
- head pounding
- skin getting sweaty or clammy
- throat constricting
- body hairs standing on end
- goosebumps forming
- head getting light
- voice getting louder and faster
- neck or head hurting

> Our anger's journey can be very complicated. But it is certainly worth taking the trouble to become familiar with our own particular set of filters and responses because that is the first step towards having more control.
> **Gael Lindenfield, from *Managing Anger: Simple Steps to Dealing with Frustration and Threat* (Thorsons, 2000)**

Take a deep breath

Deep breathing is one of the simplest ways to calm down. When we get angry or stressed, it kick-starts a physiological reaction in our bodies as the so-called 'stress hormones', adrenaline and cortisol, are released in our bodies. Our heart starts to beat faster, our blood pressure rises and our breathing becomes shallow.

Simple breathing techniques can help to reverse all those things and go a long way to calming us down physically. They also give you something to concentrate on, other than the situation that's bothering you. And you can do them any time, anywhere, for an instantly soothing effect.

"Deep breathing's something I often recommend," says Angela Rhydderch. "It's an effective way to split your anger in two. The breathing helps both to calm the physical symptoms and distract your mind from the situation you're in – just until you're more able to make sense of them."

How to do it

Key to deep breathing is the use of the diaphragm, or lower chest muscle, to allow full expansion of the lungs. The best way to work out whether you're doing this is to place a hand on your chest and a hand on your abdomen. You want your abdomen to move when you breathe in and out, not your chest. Breathe in as far as possible, through your nose, and slowly exhale through the mouth, letting every bit of air out that you can.

It's a fantastically useful skill to have under your belt – not only can it help you through any number of specific tricky situations (and not just the ones the kids land you in, either) but if you set aside a regular slot to work on it, it's a great method of relaxation generally.

You could try something as simple as pausing, and taking three very long, slow breaths. Or you could try one of the tips and techniques below.

- Take longer to breathe out than in. Count for seven seconds in and 11 out (this is a technique known as 7-11 – it's nothing to do with corner shops, though.) You can also use a five-in and nine-out count, if that's easier.
- Focus on feeling grounded, or as though you have a 'strong core' inside you. Imagine your breath is coming from your feet all the way up your body and out of your mouth.
- Try repeating a word quietly to yourself as you breathe. (Preferably something like 'calm' or 'peace' – even if you do have a more colourful word in mind.)
- Roar as you exhale. (And then enjoy the look on your kids' faces).

> Once you have truly regained your emotional equilibrium you can decide at leisure what you think is best to do about the situation rather than letting your anger tell you.
> **William Davies, from *Overcoming Anger and Irritability* (Constable and Robinson, 2000)**

Other ways to calm down are the breathing exercises you're supposed to do during childbirth – really good for just giving a minute to take stock and not go over the edge. Going outside

> and walking round the garden helps too, as does dancing! We put on some loud music and we all dance – it does defuse a situation and helps me to see the bigger picture.
> **Antonia, mum to kids aged seven, three and eight months**

Muscular relaxation

This is another good way of releasing built-up tension and slowing down an adrenaline rush in the heat of the moment: the idea is to work on tense muscles by first clenching them tightly and then relaxing them. It's also a good thing to try at the end of a difficult day or a week, to help you to relax. If you've got the luxury of time you can work on all the muscle groups in turn. But if you're in a spot of bother, you could just concentrate on a handful of the most tension-prone areas – try twisting your neck to the side as far as possible, relaxing, and repeating the other side. Or pull your shoulders tight up to your ears, hold for a few seconds, and then let them drop. Do this slowly and gently, though, to avoid straining anything.

Seek some inner peace, man

It's not just for hippies – meditation is good for cross parents, too. In case you didn't know, meditation is all about freeing your mind from negative feelings by quiet contemplation and reflection.

I can't claim to know much about this ancient practice, and I suspect you need to put in a fair amount of time and commitment to achieving real inner peace this way. But in its simplest form, a spot of meditation can be tremendously helpful when the heat is on.

Close your eyes, breathe deeply, and focus: not on whatever it is that's making you cross, frustrated, or stressed out, but something positive instead.

Back down to earth

'Grounding' is another useful technique which can help a cross person re-focus emotions and come back from whatever level of crisis they've reached to the 'here and now'.

"It's a way of pulling back from the emotional mind to a more thought-out, reasonable mind which will help us make better decisions," explains psychologist Dr Angharad Rudkin.

There are all sorts of simple and useful grounding techniques worth trying when you can feel yourself edging towards explosion – splashing your face with cold water, for example, wiggling your fingers in front of your eyes, and taking a moment to look around at your physical surroundings, concentrating carefully on everything you can see, hear and smell.

Seeing something different

In a stressful situation you can sometimes close your eyes and imagine yourself out of it by employing a little 'imagery'. Think of a time or place where you know you'll be happy. If you can conjure up sounds and smells that help whisk you away, so much the better.

Other uses of imagery include 'visualising' your anger or stress as a means of getting rid of it. If you can summon up a picture of the rumbling force inside you, you may also be able to conjure a vision of it leaving your body and taking all those negative vibes away with it. An example is seeing it as a cloud of black smoke, which you can push out of your body as you breathe out.

And yes, I realise much of the above sounds a tad weird – but these techniques really *can* be effective. Give them a go some time.

[*There are some useful references for further sources of relaxation, deep breathing and meditation techniques listed on the White Ladder Press website. More details at the end of the book.*]

Think about *why* you are angry

OK, so there may not be time for a full-blown analysis of the situation when you're in the midst of a paddy, but it's good if you can use that 'pause for thought' moment to think about why you're feeling angry. It may help you to establish whether or not the situation is worth getting really riled about at all. And if there's something more fundamental bothering you and affecting your tolerance, you need to work out what it is so you can tackle it.

The power of positive thought

Now, it's true that this is not easy to put into practice if either your children (or you) are in a particularly Satanic mood – and nigh on impossible if you've already entered the realms of fury. But in the build-up to a blow-out, concentrating on what you love about them, and how adorable they are when they're asleep/just out of the bath/on their best behaviour, can sometimes help when what you're actually thinking is how much you'd like to put them up for adoption.

There's a technique in psychology and anger management called 're-framing' , and it means trying to look at a situation from a different perspective and seeing anything good or positive that you can in it. Now, it has to be said that there is many an angry moment in family life that even New Labour's finest would struggle to put a positive spin on. For instance, there's probably not much point in trying to tell yourself what a free-spirited creative genius your child is because they've just left a marker pen 'design' on the sitting room carpet. (Although you *might* be able to tell yourself that you needed an incentive to get it professionally cleaned, anyway.)

But this strategy can be effective. A little example: my older daughter has an unbelievably annoying habit of pulling on my wrist, hard, while I'm pushing her younger sister in the buggy. It hurts, and it makes pushing the buggy even harder. But I often 're-frame' this situation by reminding myself that this is her way of keeping some physical contact with me when I don't have a spare hand for her to hold. Which makes it seem less annoying, and actually quite sweet.

Another example: sometimes, when I walk into a room and it looks as though it has been comprehensively dismantled by a team of demolition experts, I stop for a moment and think about how the mess my house is in reflects the joyful, active lives that are lived in it – and how miserably pristine it would be if I'd never been blessed with children.

A little positive thought can go a long way. If you have a friend unlucky enough to be without kids because of fertility problems, dwell for a moment on how they'd give their eye teeth to experience parenthood – even the crappy bits. Imagine being a mother to a starving child in Africa – now *that* would be bad. It may sound sentimental, but counting your blessings is a good thing to do when you can't remember quite what is so blessed about the little devil who has expressed their creativity, indelibly, on your carpet.

And if you can't buy that, well, fair enough. Have a glass of wine, instead (and please read the next chapter before you start arguing with me about using alcohol as a prop).

Put yourself in their shoes

It can be incredibly hard to empathise with children when their behaviour is unfathomable. But – as Yoda would no doubt have put it – empathise you must.

Remember that list of reasons why kids are so infuriating, in Chapter 1? In most cases, there'll be a rational explanation, emotional or practical, for their behaviour when they're doing something that winds us up. At times of trouble it can really help to spend a moment identifying what that may be, considering it a while, and then empathising with them just as hard as you can.

Periods of challenging behaviour usually come and go, and some parents find that the mantra 'it's just a phase' is a useful one. It's one reason why subsequent children can be less maddening than your first – you know with certainty that they'll eventually cease the annoying tendencies they're displaying during that particular part of their lives. (The fact that they'll inevitably swap it for an annoying behaviour of a different sort is neither here nor there.)

> When my temper is frayed, I try hard to see the situation from a different angle. I remind myself this is a small, often tired, child who is struggling to cope with whatever life is throwing at them. For example, when we are running late for school and I'm getting angry because my daughter ignores my tenth request to get her shoes on, I try to remember that she knows I'm taking her brother to her favourite music group that morning, and how unfair that must feel.
>
> **Charlotte, mum to kids aged four and two**

When the shoes are much bigger (and smellier)

Empathy is an especially necessary skill for parents of adolescents and teenagers. Just as, with toddlers, you need to put yourself in their irrational, frustrated little shoes, with teens you need to remind yourself when they piss you off that it's practically in their job description to do so. And whilst they may have acquired the power of rational thought by then, they have much the same frustrations as little kids – there's so much they want to do, yet so much of it they can't.

It can help to draw on your (quite possibly painful) memories of your own youth. Unless you were one of the Waltons, you'll no doubt have made your own parents angry with your shenanigans, and unless you've had a complete memory lapse, you'll recall how you felt about that. When the going gets tough with your teen, remind yourself how it feels to be one: confusing, scary, exciting, insecure.

Compromise is everything at this age, so if you're too cross to even contemplate negotiation, put a bit of time and space between you before attempting to thrash things out, and wait until you're totally calm before you do so. While you pause, don't forget to put yourself in their trainers.

> It helps sometimes just remembering what it is like to be a teenager. I hated that feeling of being in between, not being a child but not being an adult either.
> **Emma, mum to kids aged 17 and 14**

When your button is pushed by your child's behaviour, think about his intention beneath the behaviour. See if you can get past the He's Doing That Just to Get to Me perception to What does the behaviour mean, and how can I help him? Consider that your child has a problem, instead of making *him* the problem.
From *When Your Kids Push Your Buttons*, by Bonnie Harris (Warner Books, 2003)

PARENTS' PANEL: Do you ever use positive thought to get yourself through a negative moment?

One thing I always do whenever there's been discord in the family – go into them at night, take a deep breath of all that is my children and watch their sleeping faces, which always look the same as they did when they were little babes. (Admittedly, this might stop during the teenage years.)

No matter what they've done they look so gorgeous when they're asleep, so little and so vulnerable. Also, they can't answer back and it gives you a sneaky chance to win the argument that they wouldn't let you win earlier.

You have to be very quiet though. I have unintentionally scared the living daylights out of them when they've woken suddenly to see a dark figure lurking by their bedside!
Helen, mum to sons aged 10 and seven

What I find helps is trying to wait a second before I reply or shout – it gives me time to think about how much I love her and makes me slightly more patient.
Jane, mum to kids aged four and five months

I hate it when they disintegrate into tears or a tantrum at the slightest thing. But I usually try and think about the way they are feeling and put myself in their situation. (In most cases it breaks your heart!)
Andy, dad to daughters aged six and three

Perspective is key. Focus on how great children really are. Imagine being a mum in Africa – life expectancy is about 35, I think, in some places. And I remind myself they're not young for long. Time passes so quickly.
Alison, mum to kids aged seven, five and two

Last year my husband had to go away on a five-week business

trip. Whenever I was feeling stressed, I thought of a mum I'd known who'd died of cancer a few months previously. Her boys were aged five and seven. I imagined what she wouldn't give to spend five weeks on her own with her children. Certainly a case of counting my blessings.
Juliet, mum to kids aged eight, six and three

This might sound a bit frilly, but when he's being a terror, I try and stay focused on how cute he is normally, and tell myself over again that this current mood will blow over and he will be cute again at some point.
Alison, mum to a son aged two

I find myself constantly gazing at the beautiful photos of my children in my house. I need to do this sometimes to remind myself (when they are both whinging or crying or running off into the distance) of the fact that they are amazing children and I really am very lucky.
Helen, mum to kids aged five and two

Whenever the kids hit out and I think that they really hate me, I remind myself it's because, not despite, the fact that we are so close. They are so lovely with other people and are good company almost all the time. It's only us as parents that suffer and that's fine. I'd rather they were grotty with us and sweetness and light with everyone else than the other way round.
Emma, mum to kids aged 17 and 15

I have to admit that I let things go if I know my daughter is under stress from other aspects of her life, studying for exams perhaps, or maybe trouble with relationships. (Also, rather selfishly, I don't have a go if I am due a favour from her, like babysitting.)
Nick, dad to kids aged 17 and 10

I tell myself all the time that this is just a phase and it won't last for ever.
Judy, mum to sons aged three and one

ANGER MANAGEMENT: top tips from experts

Number three: The 'One Point' Technique

Stand straight, with your legs apart so you have a solid base – imagine your feet are like the roots of an old oak tree (very wise and solid). Stand up tall and take three breaths. Then move your attention to or put your hand on the place just below your tummy button – this is the centre of balance in your body, the 'one point' (it's also known as the Hara Point in martial arts). Try looking at the situation from this calm, centred place where you're rooted and in control.
From *Raising Happy Kids for Dummies*, by Sue Atkins (Wiley, 2007)

4

Time out for grown-ups

> When our children provoke unrecognisable depths of anger and hostility, we have to dig deep into our reserves of self-restraint in order not to be found guilty of manslaughter.
> **Kate Figes, from *Life After Birth* (Viking, 1998)**

I'm outta here

Walking away is a perfectly acceptable response when you're so cross you can't trust yourself to be near the small person or people who've provoked you. It stands to reason: if you're no longer in the same vicinity, you cannot let rip in ways which you regret later.

Parenting experts approve more or less universally of the 'time out' technique – physically removing a child from a situation and leaving them elsewhere for a while to cool down. And it *is* helpful, but you really need to be feeling cool *yourself* to carry it out successfully. If you're seething when you remove them to their bedroom – or wherever – the temptation may be to manhandle them there. So sometimes it's better to put *yourself* in another room and take that 'time out' yourself.

There are a number of variations on the theme, but usually it's just a question of removing yourself from the room. Some people prefer to move to a different floor, others into the garden or garage – clearly, if the kids you're leaving behind are little, you need to make sure you don't go anywhere far, or for long.

> The wonderful thing about saying nothing is that you never have to take it back.
> **Nancy Samalin, from *Love and Anger: The Parental Dilemma***

Isn't that a cop-out?

Purists might argue that you walk away at your peril because it's effectively backing down from the situation, and to a confrontational child that may feel a lot like victory. So be it. My personal feeling is that *sometimes*, it's better to cop out than to freak out.

You can minimise the indignity of ducking out by making clear that you're not giving up on the situation, you just can't handle it at that moment. Preface your disappearance with a brief disclaimer, for example: "I am so cross, I cannot trust myself to be near you, so I'm going to walk away. We will continue the discussion when I'm calm again." And then, of course, you need to go back as promised and seek a satisfactory conclusion – after you've breathed deeply, imbibed a cup of coffee, kicked the fridge, or whatever it takes to calm down again.

"Of course it's OK to walk away sometimes," reassures Dr Angharad Rudkin. "You're not in competition with your children. If you worry about who's won what, then you'll be spending a lot of time as a parent feeling frustrated. As long as you share a big kiss goodnight at the end of the day, there are no losers."

Do something nice instead

If you can find yourself a pleasant little distraction during your walk-out, so much the better. Admittedly, it may not be a practical option to take yourself off for a leisurely, ylang ylang-scented foam bath, or lock yourself in the sitting room for an hour while you catch up on the EastEnders omnibus. But speedy, smaller indulgences can be soothing: a piece of chocolate, a breath of fresh air, a glass of wine* (see later), or your favourite song on the stereo. Whatever dings your dong.

Bye bye, baby

Even as tiny babies, our children bring out the extremes of emotion in us – no bad thing, as it's useful preparation for the rollercoaster years ahead. The challenges of the early months can certainly knock a parent's sanity for six, what with the relentless demands of these tiny little humans, their sometimes unstinting bouts of crying, and their often steadfast refusal to sleep properly at night. You don't even get much back for your troubles, apart from the odd toothless grin. Knackered and taken for granted, it's hardly surprising that our parental anger triggers can be sparked mere weeks into our children's lives.

It's absolutely fine to employ the 'time out for grown-ups' techniques on babies and very young children if they drive you to it, with one obvious disclaimer: you need to be satisfied they're safe before you leave them. If they still haven't got control of their limbs, then you'll be fine just leaving them on the floor, but if they're rolling over, crawling or up on their feet, you need to make sure they're safe in a cot or a playpen or strapped firmly into a buggy or bouncy seat before doing a runner.

They may well cry even harder if you walk out on them. But they will be *absolutely fine* without you for a few moments. And if the alternative is you scaring or even hurting them as a result of your inflamed temper, then you'll be taking the better option.

"It's a very normal to feel upset or angry in this sort of situation, especially if you're stressed generally, because a baby's cry is designed to make you react. It's the way you react, though, that's important," assures Maggie Fisher, a professional officer for the Community Practitioners' and Health Visitors' Association. "I think that when you've got to the stage where you think you might blow your top, you need to put the baby down, check the room, and go and take five. If possible, put some music on. It really can get to you and sometimes you need to put a bit of distance between you and the child, so you can re-group and calm down before going back in. If it's really bad, phone a friend and ask them to take the baby out for 10 minutes. Or phone a helpful advice line such as Cry-sis or Parentline Plus – sometimes it can really help just talking to a sane, calm adult at these moments."

[*Details for these and other advice lines, and some suggestions for further reading on this subject, can be found on the White Ladder Press website.*]

> The most memorable time was when he was maybe five or six weeks old. I was seriously sleep-deprived and had moved jobs and country. In fact I was probably a bit psychotic. He had colic and would not sleep or stop crying, and I found myself thumping the carpeted floor because the alternative was to thump him.
> **Paul, dad to a son aged two**
>
> When she was first born, postnatal depression meant I would sit in another room while she howled and I tried to concentrate on not just leaving the flat. It did help, just to give me enough time to listen to her, to remember she's a child, and that she needs me, to pull myself together. It's easier to be loving when you're calm.
> **Verity, mum to a daughter aged one**
>
> I have shut the door and gone outside once or twice, just to get

> away from the screaming. It helps my head to clear and helps me calm down, so I can go back in and try again.
> **Laura, mum to twins aged six months**

Postnatal depression

Feelings of despair and irritability during the first year or so of motherhood may be linked to postnatal depression (PND). The causes of PND are unclear and subject to much debate – some say hormonal changes are most likely to be to blame, others that it's more likely a reaction to the shock of such a demanding new role, hampered by one or more other stresses in life.

Statistics suggest that up to 15 per cent of women suffer from PND, although some experts believe it to be more widespread, and as many as 80 per cent are reckoned to experience the much milder and shorter-lived 'baby blues', which tends to last a matter of days. Men may well suffer from PND, too: certainly, there's little doubt that dads can also feel the strain in the difficult first months of a baby's life.

Depending on the severity, PND can be treated with either medication or counselling, or it may go away on its own, with the aid of lots of practical and emotional support, and plenty of rest.

A health visitor or GP will always take any concerns you have about PND extremely seriously, so they should be your first port of call if you are worried. Talking to someone who cares is also a vital step. If there's no one around who you feel you could turn to, log on to a website like ***www.netmums.com*** *for online friendship and advice.*

There's some useful contact details and links to more information about this subject on the White Ladder Press website – more information at the back of the book.

Toddling off

Ah, toddlerdom. The age at which children discover their parents *have* a response button – and that pushing it can have all sorts of interesting effects.

The tears and tantrums that come as a matter of course with this age group are not displays of naughtiness – really! They're just normal ways for little kids to push boundaries, gain attention and communicate the frustrations they feel about their own limitations. And this sort of behaviour is *definitely* just a phase, albeit one you may have to endure for several years. If you can 'reframe' the situation by reminding yourself of these things, put yourself in their shoes and imagine how it feels, or draw on all your powers of positive thought to get you through these challenging moments, then by all means do.

Sometimes, throwing a tantrum right back at them seems like the only option available. But really, this kind of response is best avoided because it's not going to make you – or the kid – feel any better about the situation.

"The last thing a child who's out of control needs is a parent who's out of control, too," says Maggie Fisher, of the Community Practitioners' and Health Visitors' Association. "They're struggling to manage their feelings and, ideally, they need a calm adult around them to help them do that."

A spot of 'time out' for the small person in question is what's usually prescribed here by the experts, or of course, there's that classic piece of advice to bend down and hold them tight until the rage subsides. Neither strategy is much help to a parent who is themselves so overheated they are likely to physically throw them into their bedroom, or hold them so tight it hurts. If you don't think you can trust yourself to react calmly, your best bet is to take your own little bit of time out.

It's also OK to do this with a pre-schooler, but if they're past the age where you can restrain them in a cot, playpen or high chair, you clearly can't go far, or for long, in case they hurt themselves. Just outside the door is probably a good place. And aim to leave them for no longer than two minutes – if you want to work on a calming-down strategy, you'll have to do so sharpish.

"If you can, let them get on with it. Small children naturally tend to explode and release all their feelings which is healthy and normal," says Maggie Fisher. "And we all lose it sometimes, too, but it's better if we don't lose it alongside them. If they're having a tantrum, walk out and leave them. In fact, it's better if they don't have an audience – they'll often pick themselves up and the tantrum will be over more quickly if you deprive them of that."

If you're reluctant to walk out of the room altogether because you're concerned about safety – perhaps because objects are flying or there are other young children in the room – then you'll have to stick around. But any amount of space in between you and the kid can be helpful. Take a step backwards, or turn your back on them if need be. Put your fingers in your ears and sing. Or put your head in the nearest cupboard and breathe deeply.

It goes without saying that if you're not at home – or at least in a home they know well – when things kick off, you don't really have the walking-away option. Leaving them alone in a strange place could really frighten them.

> I've yet to get my son to sit on the naughty step and actually stay there. So instead I tell him to stay in the sitting room whilst I sit in the kitchen with a coffee – the doors are open so I can see and hear him. He can't stand me being in another room and keeps following me but I tell him to go back, and he does. My husband walked in on one such occasion and was told, "Mummy's in the kitchen because I've been naughty."
> **Claire, mum to a son aged three**

A word about booze*

It's amazing, once you start talking to other parents, how many of them will admit to reaching for the bottle before *their kids' bedtime because it de-stresses them. That's because alcohol is a relaxant. Taken in moderation, it can make us feel great.*

Many experts seem opposed to the use of alcohol as an antidote to stress and anger because too much of it can affect your mood for the worse. Many would also, no doubt, argue that if you drink to calm your nerves when your children are around it's setting a poor example.

Well, obviously *it's never a good idea to be falling down drunk in charge of children. But in my (completely unqualified) opinion, there's absolutely nothing wrong with a couple of cheeky beverages knocked back before the kids' bedtime if it helps you to be a cool, calm parent during moments when you're threatening not to be.*

Some say you should wait until a decent time of day before doing so. It's widely debated among parents – and particularly among mums who are at home in the afternoon – as to what is an acceptable time to reasonably crack one open. I wouldn't like to issue a precise guideline on when the watershed – or 'wine o'clock', as a friend of a friend calls it – might be. Let's just say that in my house, it's generally 6pm. On a bad day, five.

Whether it's setting your kids the right example or not remains a matter for debate. Some might say that by uncorking a bottle of vino at the end of a stressful day you're passing on unwise

---

* Official advice is for women to stick to a daily limit of two to three units, and for men, three to four. And don't forget, a unit may be smaller than you think.

messages about the nature of booze as a 'prop' and steering them towards an alcopop-addled youth. Others would argue that, as they do on the continent, there's nothing wrong in showing your kids that limited amounts of carefully consumed alcohol can be a civilised and relaxing thing. It's your call.

Obviously, if booze in any quantity makes you mouthy or unkind, you might want to think twice about that snifter. But if the worst that can happen – as in our house – is that the karaoke machine comes out, then it's hard to see where the harm is.

Sometimes it gets to 5pm and I think how my grandfather generally has a sherry about that time, so I pour myself a glass of white wine and it really makes that time of day (tea, bath, bed) so much easier to handle.
Hannah, mum to a son aged 16 months

I couldn't survive without a big fat glass of wine at around 6pm, sometimes earlier. It does help.
Antonia, mum to kids aged seven, three and eight months

If desperate, yes, I do resort to a lunchtime glass of wine. It takes the edge off and makes things you were finding infuriating 10 minutes ago seem funny or irrelevant.
Charlotte, mum to kids aged four and two

I usually wind down with a glass of wine in the evenings – or at my daughter's tea-time, if it's been an especially bad day.
Jane, mum to kids aged four and five months

Bringing in reinforcements

A variation on the time out for grown-ups theme is 'swappsies' (not a technical term, but it seems to sum up this approach pretty well). It's what happens when you walk away and your other half – or any other available adult for that matter – takes over instead.

Lone parents (and, indeed, parents whose other-halves aren't actually around that much) may not often have this option available to them. If possible, have a relative, neighbour or good friend on speed dial for moments when you need some back-up.

> We have an 'agreement' that, if one adult perceives that the other is 'losing it' they step in, the first adult exits and the second continues in a more gentle tone. This works well the vast majority of the time.
> **Steve, dad to kids aged seven, five, and two**
>
> At times of stress I call either of my friends, who are single parents like me, or my mum. Just a chat on the phone to them helps calm me down. I do walk away sometimes, too. You have to. When it gets really bad I resent being on my own and having to deal with it all, but I get on with it.
> **Sarah, mum to a daughter aged five**
>
> The other day my son's evil twin got up. He complained and whinged all through breakfast, he wanted to go in the shower and then changed his mind, he knocked his juice all over the floor because he was messing about. All little things, I know, but when it's accompanied by a whiny cry every time you ask him to do something, it's annoying. By the time my hubby got up, I was ready to explode. So I left him with his dad and went to the newsagents.
> **Giselle, mum to a son aged four**

PARENTS' PANEL: Do you ever walk away if your kids are driving you mad?

Shutting myself in the toilet and pretending to everyone that I'm badly constipated gives me enough time to read another chapter of one of the many toddler taming books I have, to reflect, to escape and feel refreshed, and, if I *am* actually constipated, return a few pounds lighter.
Sharrone, mum to kids aged four, two and three months

I walk away sometimes. I don't normally shut the door, but I will tell my daughter I don't want to be in her company when she's behaving in a certain way, which usually does the trick. Sometimes I'll go out for a walk, if my husband is around to cover. Failing that, I might sneak round the back of the house and have a fag.
Nina, mum to kids aged four and on

I do feel my blood boiling occasionally and it helps taking myself outside of the situation so I often walk away – to the kitchen, or just outside my front door. It stops me from really shouting. I take a few deep breaths and after a few seconds I'm able to handle the situation again.
Maria, mum to a son aged four

To calm down I have to walk away and I ask my son to walk away, too. He'll go one way, I go the other, then we agree to meet in 20 minutes' time, once we've had time to calm down and reflect on what has happened. I feel this really works.
Lynne, mum to sons aged 22, 20 and 13

If my kids have made me really mad I do 'time out' for myself. Luckily my kids are old enough to realise when I've had enough, and to leave me alone. They're quite happy to amuse themselves in their rooms or garden while I retreat to the bedroom/bath-

room/front room. I find having regular breaks from them is a good de-stresser.
Rosie, mum to sons aged 11 and five

I escape and have a hot soak in the bath or go to my bedroom, shut the door and have thinking time. If I'm in a really bad way I might try a little meditation.
Nick, dad to kids aged 17 and 10

If I think I am going to lose my temper, I always walk away into another room. I just check they are safe and then wait until I'm calm again.
Jen, mum to boys aged three and nine months

I try and walk away from my kids but they always follow me. The other day I shut myself in the car (parked on the drive with a good view in to the sitting room) just to make a phone call in peace.
Kelly, mum to kids aged six, four and three

Sometimes. I try to do it before I lose my temper, though. I sit outside on the patio with a cup of tea and ignore them for 10 minutes and if it's wet and that's not an option, just going into the back room and shutting the door for a few minutes normally does the trick – so long as I know they are safe. Now there's a new baby around I do it less as I can't really just leave her.
Sharron, mum to daughters aged six, three and six months

I find that a few minutes with some kind of barrier between me and the kids, slumped in a chair with a coffee whilst reminding myself to do things slowly and carefully when I return, is best for me.
Bill, dad to a son aged three and twins aged 10 months

ANGER MANAGEMENT: top tips from experts

Number four: The FLOW Technique:

- **F is for focus** Keep your feet firmly on the ground, and focus your attention on the simple act of breathing slowly in and out.
- **L is for listen and learn** Concentrate on what the other person is saying, it helps to keep you 'present' and allows them to get their side across.
- **O is for objectivity** Stop, think and take a look at the bigger picture. Don't take what they're doing or saying personally.
- **W is for wait** Contain your feelings whilst in the heat of the moment. It pays to wait.

From '*Beating Anger*' by Mike Fisher (Rider, 2005)

5

Mind your language

> No one pushes our buttons like our children. No one knows our buttons as intimately as they do. No one can make us soar to our heights or bring us to our knees more quickly than they can.
> **Bonnie Harris, from *When Your Kids Push Your Buttons* (Warner Books Inc, 2003)**

It's not what you say

OK, so you can't overlook the problem, deep breathing ain't helping, and you're damned if you're going to walk away. There's no getting round it – you're gonna blow.

At times like these, it's a question of damage limitation. One thing you might want to do here is be mindful of how you communicate with your children because what you say and how you say it is really relevant in this business of expressing anger the right way, ie *positively, healthily and effectively*.

Of course, it's not easy in the heat of the moment to control what comes out of our mouths. Virtually all of us say things we regret sometimes, and there's very little point in feeling bad about it. There's more about that in Chapter Eight, Happy Endings.

Meanwhile, though, there are lots of ways we can consciously aim to communicate our cross feelings in positive ways – and avoid communicating them in negative ways.

Softly, softly

When tempers flare and adrenaline flows, voices tend to get louder and faster. If you concentrate hard on keeping your voice low and slow, it will help you make your point without actually getting hysterical about it. It also helps you to be clear about what you're saying and what you're hoping to get out of the situation, which can be useful as it's very easy to slip into gobbledegook mode when you're angry. And if you bring down the volume and speed of your own voice, they're less likely to shout back at you.

> Calm is infectious and spreads to those around, so for peace in life let us aim to keep the decibels down.
> **Christopher Green, from *Toddler Taming* (Vermilion, 1992)**

Don't get personal

There may well be times when you feel so angry and upset with your children that you find yourself disliking them thoroughly. When this happens, you have to remind yourself that it's just an emotionally charged blip – and that it's the behaviour you hate, not the child.

Children are very sensitive to very personal or critical language, especially when it comes from the people they need unconditional approval from the most: their mum or dad. Apart from hurting their feelings, that kind of language – used regularly – could seriously damage their self-esteem and that could have a negative impact on your relationship with them.

Of course, you may well have an important point to make to them or you may need to pull them up or tell them off. But launching into a huge verbal offensive isn't the best way forward – not least because they'll be too busy trying to shut it out to absorb any useful messages from it.

"When you do lose it and you scream at your child and say something awful, I think you can get away with it once in a while," says Nancy Samalin. "But not too much. That sort of thing is hurtful to a child because they need to feel that no matter what you do, you're still able to love them. If you've said something very hurtful, then you have to go back to your child and make sure that they know you are sorry and that you didn't mean it."

One way to work on positively expressing your thoughts that lots of experts recommend is to try using the word 'I' instead of 'You'. So, instead of: "You're a nightmare!" or "You're so naughty," try: "I'm not happy with the way you're speaking to me," or "I'm really angry about the way you're behaving."

This is a lot easier on paper than in practice, but it's something worth aiming for. (And do please note, this piece of advice *isn't* a licence to say "You're a f***ing little toe-rag," as long as you preface it with the phrase "I think ...")

Doing what it says on the label

Be cautious about labelling your kids in anger, even if they do show tendencies that repeat themselves. Tell a child they are something often enough, then that something may become set in stone. And don't bang on about their bad behaviour in the past – it's pointless and it will only make you feel more resentful. Keep focused on whatever it is that's making you cross at the time.

Are you threatening me?

Don't let a lost temper compel you to issue threats that you can't possibly (and wouldn't want to) back up. If you warn them of a consequence, you need to be able to carry it through if any of your future warnings are going to be heeded – so screaming that you intend to lock them in their bedroom without food or water for the next fortnight is pretty pointless.

Children often misunderstand or take literally adults' comments, even those made without genuine intent. If the words, "I'm putting you in a children's home," for example, or "That's it – I'm leaving," come tumbling out, then you may need to retract them – smartish.

As Angharad Rudkin puts it: "Children have quite enough scares in their little worlds as it is (monsters and all that), and anyway, threatening them yourself is going to get you nowhere. It may make them scared and back down for a little while, but fear is not a good long-term strategy for managing someone, because very soon they're going to learn that you don't mean a word. And then when you tell them you're sending them to the children's home they'll simply say: 'I don't care if you send me to the children's home. Anywhere would be better than here'!"

Stop *@"*ing swearing!

Kids can provoke the demurest of parents to descend to navvy-like levels of expression. I write this with one hand, as the other is firmly up in the air just now. I'm afraid that, even though I know it is neither big, nor clever, I am often to be heard barking very rude words indeed within earshot of my daughters.

Well now, that said, I must dutifully report that swearing *in front* of your kids isn't really ideal, mainly because it's not what you'd call 'modelling good manners'. Inevitably – at some point – they'll repeat what they hear and it may be at school, in front of Auntie Maureen, or directly at you. And you'll hardly be able to complain about it.

There is a good deal of release to be had from saying something rude out loud, it has to be said, and you can get *some* satisfaction from pseudo-swearing. Fiddlesticks! Shucks! and For crying out loud! are all reasonable alternatives, if you say them loudly enough. Another possibility is to do your swearing in another room.

Of course, context is everything. If you're actually swearing *at* them, or if you combine swearing with loudly dealt criticism or very hurtful remarks, that's not good. If you just happen to release a string of expletives into the air as a general expression of how mad you are, well, that's rather more understandable.

I suppose I would say that.

> My youngest was whining for her milk, it was really early in the morning and I hadn't had much sleep. In fact, I don't think I lost it with her as much as with the situation; too early, too tired, spilt milk, whiny infant and then the final straw, she complained that it wasn't warm enough. I threw a milk cup at the fridge and I called the microwave a c**t. All in all, it wasn't a good start to the day.
> **Andy, dad to daughters aged six and three**

Be grown-up about it

'Don't take it personally' is a basic tenet of anger management, and it's particularly relevant where kids are concerned because rarely do our children truly intend to hurt us – even the stroppy teenage sorts – with the things they say. It can help to remind yourself of this when the temptation to verbally retaliate looms.

"If they say something bad to you, you have to tell yourself that they're not deliberately being unkind or vicious," says Sue Atkins, parenting coach and author of *Raising Happy Kids for Dummies (Wiley, 2007)*. "A lot of the time, they're only little people making mistakes."

In fact, if you try hard enough you can actually see the positive side in it when they say awful things to you.

"Even if they're trying to hurt you, it's only because they feel safe enough with you to be able to do that and know that you still love them," says Angharad Rudkin. "In fact – that's a perfect example of how the re-framing technique [see page 43] can work.'

Keep telling yourself: *they* are the child, and *you* are the adult. Aim to come up with an answer to whatever they throw at you that illustrates just how mature you are, and then wallow in the satisfaction that brings. The NSPCC suggests this example: if they say "I hate you Mum," say: "That's a shame, because I really love you." (I know it ain't easy being cheesy. But it's worth a try.)

Hear them out

Don't make it a one-sided rant. As soon as they're old enough to talk, they're entitled to an opinion and listening to it is another useful way of pressing that pause button and giving yourself a chance to catch your own breath. Parenting experts emphasise the importance of communicating with our kids, and that includes allowing them to speak and listening to what they've got to say, always.

"If you don't listen then what you're saying is that their opinion doesn't count," says Sue Atkins. "You're saying, 'I'm the parent and I'm older and I know better than you'. And that goes for any age group, although it gets more and more important to hear them out the older they get. You have to find a balance, yes, because you are the adult, and you may well know better than them. But it's also important to listen without interruption. It's about showing them respect, and building their own self-respect by hearing them and allowing them to be heard. And if you stop to get their side of things, then you've got the whole picture, not just your half of it."

Dr Rudkin agrees. "One sure way to wind someone up is by not listening to them. So, if you're serious about not wanting to get into a big argument make sure *you* listen to *them*. You can always pre-empt it by saying, 'I'm going to speak first and I want you to listen. When I have finished my bit, you can talk and I promise I will listen without interrupting,'" she advises.

All that said, there's no reason why you should have to give your attention to a child who's being rude or abusive towards you, or is shouting so loudly they're not making much sense anyway. In these circumstances, let them know you'll hear them out but only when things are calmer. And if you need to at that point, take a moment to remind yourself that there's nothing to be gained from shouting back at them.

Be specific

Children respond a lot better when they know exactly what it is that you're cross about, so always try and be specific in your ranting.

As Sue Atkins explains: "'Tidy your room' is too vague. They're not mind readers, they're kids. They need to know exactly what you want them to do and why. So, not: 'Tidy the bathroom.' but 'See that towel, if you pick it up and hang it up it will be dry when you need it tomorrow'. And that's relevant from toddler to teens."

Teen talk

Emotions run high in the teenage years. They're sensitive souls and their self-esteem can be fragile. Conversely, this is the time (given that they will usually be boundary-pushing for England, under pressure from all angles, and at the mercy of their hormones) when they're most likely to give you a mouthful that you'd love nothing better than to return.

Here are a few things to remember when a teenager is making you mad:

Avoid hectoring and lecturing. Don't bang on about it. They'll probably get the point first time (unless they *actually* have their fingers in their ears and are saying "la la la" very loudly). And steer clear of personal criticism. Remember, they're sensitive souls, even if they do go around pretending not to care about anything.

Empathise till it hurts. Try to remind yourself that they have a lot on their plate – exams, hormones, peer pressure, the opposite sex, among other things.

Aim to rise above them if they insult you. It's unlikely they have truly hurtful intentions. Just like toddlers (but less cute), they are pushing the boundaries as a test of your love. It can (though won't necessarily) help you to re-frame a situation by reminding yourself of that.

Listening to them is more important than talking to them at this stage in their lives. Don't forget to make it clear that you are listening to them and – crucially – have actually heard what they're saying.

> I'm going through a difficult time with my eldest daughter at the moment. She was 13 yesterday. I understand that her hormones are all over the place and girls do get moody and irritable, but I never imagined that my sweet little girl would turn into such a she-devil. She answers back, is lazy, has serious attitude problems, and treats me like her personal assistant. She is pushing the boundaries big time.
> **Christine, mum to kids aged 13, 10 and nine**

PARENTS' PANEL: Do you ever use language you wish you hadn't?

"Mummy's not very happy with you" is a regular thing but I've also heard myself say "I don't love you any more" or "I don't want to be your friend", which I've been mortified about afterwards. I always try to have a cuddle and reinforce that I do love him but when he behaves badly it makes me sad. Unfortunately, he also tends to relate these events as stories to my parents, in-laws and husband.
Claire, mum to a son aged three

Oh yes, especially if hormonally fuelled. Early on in my fourth pregnancy, following some challenging behaviour from them, I informed the children that I hated them all and that I wasn't going to pick them up from music school because I was leaving them. The language was rather colourful, let me tell you. I dropped them off, sobbed uncontrollably in the car thinking that I was a terrible mother to say such things, and that they would be better off without me so I would move alone to France and put the new baby up for adoption. I came home and put myself to bed, and my husband picked them up later that morning. I thought they would moan about me to him, and that they would be emotionally scarred for ever, but they all came in and started tickling my feet and loving me. How cool is that? I apologised for the things I said but do you know, I don't even think they remembered. They are so secure in my love for them. It doesn't justify my behaviour though. As hard as it is, I always try to say sorry when I've over-reacted.
Ellie, mum to kids aged 11, nine, six and one month

I'm usually quite even-tempered but one incident really sticks in my mind. We were going to a daytime concert and I was really looking forward to it. The youngest was tired, so I was hoping she'd sleep in her buggy while the concert was on, and I took

her off for a walk. After half an hour of screaming, she still wouldn't sleep, wouldn't even stay in her buggy, and was scratching me. I was really tired from a very disturbed night the night before and her screaming just pushed me over the edge – I remember picking her up very roughly, turning her to face me, shouting at her that I f**king hated her. When she just screamed louder I slapped her leg (I feel dreadful just remembering it). It didn't stop her screaming, but it made me burst into tears! Fortunately my husband appeared then and he picked her up and she stopped screaming immediately. He told me to go off and have some time alone, and 10 minutes later I'd calmed down and went and found them, gave my daughter a cuddle, and apologised to her. She gave me a huge hug and promptly fell asleep on my shoulder – so I guess she didn't hold any grudges!
Maggie, mum to kids aged three and 19 months

The last time I was at meltdown (after the boys were repeatedly ignoring any instruction I gave them and were fighting and screaming continually) I told the eldest – shouted at him, in fact, horribly – that if he couldn't behave himself I would have to send him away until he learnt how to. He was sitting at the top of the stairs and burst into tears and said, "Well that's not very nice Mummy!" I then felt so guilty for scaring him and for saying such a horrible thing I immediately backtracked and ended up promising him football cards after school. I was also annoyed with myself, as I am every time I end up losing it for not handling the whole situation better ... but, well, you know how it gets.
Katy, mum to sons aged five and three

It was bedtime, we were all tired and my eldest started to mess about, refusing to get into the bath. He started crying, which set the baby off in his cot, and then the pair of them were screaming. I'd just had enough and screamed back: "Be quiet! I've had enough of both of you." I picked him up, virtually threw him into the bath, and then I sat on the floor and cried. He was so upset to see me cry, he calmed right down. The little one fell asleep and I was able to get both of them down quickly.

When my husband got home 10 minutes later, all was calm. The whole thing only lasted 20 minutes and maybe it sounds trivial, but I hate shouting at the children and it really shakes me up when I lose control.
Jen, mum to sons aged three and nine months

I've said lots of things that I regret. Firstly that monsters come out at night which is why little children have to go to bed ... paid for that one with nightmares, serves me right. When my six-year-old told me she hated me repeatedly, I told her I would phone Social Services and get her a new mummy if she hated me that much. She was horrified and I felt really, really bad. I never seem to learn with this one. I should follow my own advice always to 'think before you speak'.
Kelly, mum to kids aged six, four and three

To my eternal shame as a sleep-deprived hormonal wreck a week after the traumatic birth of my second baby, I heard myself yell at my first-born who had just woken me and the baby in a rare moment of sleep: "You are ruining this family." It still makes my blood run cold to think of it.
Lucy, mum to boys aged 10 and seven

I know it sounds piddly, but I really regret getting so cross with my kids that I swear at them. I get really embarrassed about it. I really don't think that I should be so out of control that I can't keep basic swear words in. I always apologise and explain that I was very cross and that those words are not to be used by children and that adults shouldn't even be using them.
Angila, mum to kids aged six and two

I said some terrible things the other day. I'd been up half the night and was tired – so maybe their behaviour wasn't as bad as I thought – but they'd already made me cross by throwing food on the floor. Then as I tried to make an important phone call they were climbing on me, tugging at me and shouting. I could feel my blood boiling. When I came off the phone I found they'd shredded a complete toilet roll all over the bathroom floor. Then they started whining about wanting their tea, then it was books and puzzles scattered everywhere. The youngest had even taken her dirty nappy off and left it on the floor. That did it. I shouted that they were children from hell and that I wished I'd never had them. I was picking their puzzles and books up, throwing them into bin bags and vowing to chuck them away. Eventually I calmed myself down and got them ready for bed. We cuddled up on the sofa and the eldest said she was sorry for being naughty and I said I was sorry for shouting at her. I did feel guilty. But they were very good for me for a long time afterwards.
Helen, mum to daughters aged four and one

Yes, and I have hated myself for it. The only way to make amends is to apologise and try to explain in a way that they can understand that, whatever you said, you said because you were angry and upset. You didn't mean the things you said, it's just that you were hurting inside and wanted to get rid of some of the hurt.
Christine, mum to kids aged 13, 10 and nine

I once told my son he was stupid, which I really regret as he is so wonderful. It was just in the heat of the moment.
Elizabeth, mum to kids aged seven, four and two

My husband once got so angry with my eldest, then aged seven, that he yelled, "If you keep behaving like this you're going to give me a heart attack." Two years later, during which time –

needless to say – my son didn't behave like an angel, my husband died of an unexpected heart attack. To this day I don't know if my son remembers it and, of course, I can't ask him. I just hope to God he doesn't.
Miranda, mum to sons aged 11 and five

Recently I screamed at my daughter for all I was worth. I regret it now, but weeks of winding up had to be vented at some point and that's my style. Passive 99.9% of the time ... 0.1% major explosion!
Nick, dad to kids aged 17 and 10

I try really hard not to say anything I regret, especially since she soaks up things people tell her like a sponge – she once told me that I'd said she was clumsy. She is going through a clumsy phase, it's true, but I felt really bad that this was the first thing she thought of, instead of all the times I tell her how clever/gorgeous/kind she is! If I do say something I regret then I make sure to apologise afterwards and say that I was cross, and that people say things they don't mean when they're cross. Then I always give her a hug.
Jane, mum to kids aged four and five months

ANGER MANAGEMENT: top tips from experts

Number five: The Positive Self-Talk Technique

To inoculate yourself against the rising tide of angry tension, you can engage in positive self-talk by repeating (silently or out loud) phrases such as, 'Easy does it. Don't get so upset.'

From *Anger Management for Dummies* by W. Doyle Gentry (Wiley, 2007)

6

Let's (not) get physical

> Suddenly I find myself smack in the middle of another scene with an entirely different set of characters. In fifteen seconds flat, I've been cast in the role of besieged mother. And the children! These disgusting children are nothing but a bunch of savages. The mood that made the moment before so lively and loving has vanished completely. (I can't even remember it). In its place comes a primitive longing to ATTACK! My spontaneous urge is to knock all their heads together – but I know where spontaneity will get me ...
>
> **Adele Faber and Elaine Mazlish, from *Liberated Parents, Liberated Children* (Avon, 1974, reissued 2002 by Picadilly Press)**

Hit and miss

Sometimes, in moments of extreme rage, there comes the temptation – for very many parents – to reach out and hit, slap or smack their child.

There's really nothing abnormal in *feeling* like you want to wallop, shake or chuck your children out of the window. In a blind rage, it's frightening how intense our reactions can be – even to the extent that we feel violent. The clever bit is to not actually *act* on those feelings.

"There's a big difference between what you *feel* like doing and what you end up doing. It's OK to feel you'd like to hang your child by the fingertips out the window but it's not all right to actually do it," says Nancy Samalin, author of *Love and Anger: the Parental Dilemma (Penguin, 1991).*

Smacking does happen

I do acknowledge the fact that there are plenty of ordinary, loving parents – including a number who have contributed their thoughts to this book – who choose to smack their children, and an even larger number – myself included – who make very conscious efforts not to smack but might occasionally do so if shocked, scared or sufficiently enraged into a temporary loss of resolve (and who will usually then feel terrible about it).

For the purposes of this book though, which is fundamentally about coping with our parental anger in the most positive ways we can, the message *has* to be that smacking is to be avoided. And by that I mean smacking of the light to moderate variety – it goes without saying that any more *significant* hitting or hurting cannot be part of life in a loving home.

Controversy abounds here. It's illegal now in England, Wales and Northern Ireland to hit a child beyond 'reasonable chastisement', which means in such a way that will leave a mark. (And Scotland has a similar but slightly more complex law). But the fact is that the majority of experts – as well as a large number of organisations including the NSPCC and The Children's Society – are united in their opposition to smacking of any kind. Many other countries in Europe have a total ban on smacking, and there's a fairly major campaign for one here, too.

"The problem with hitting is that you're doing harm to someone with the misconception that you are teaching them something. The other big problem is that you're modelling behaviour that you don't want them to emulate," says Nancy Samalin. "If you have a rule in your house that they don't hit their brother or sister, you have to be the first one to uphold that rule."

Parenting coach Sue Atkins backs that view. "If you're getting your parenting right and you've got support and you're not over-stressed, there are so many other things you can do before you even get to that stage," she says. "You wouldn't like it if someone came up to you and slapped you. It's physically hurting another person, and it's a lack of control. I'm not claiming to be Mother Teresa on this but it has to be that it's not acceptable."

Smacking: the bottom line

Here are some of the reasons, according to the anti-smacking lobby, that smacking isn't a good idea:

- *It passes on the message that hitting is OK and makes a child more likely to be violent towards others.*
- *As a consequence it's not actually particularly effective. It may earn you short-term compliance but is unlikely to be a useful deterrent for the future.*
- *You have to smack harder and harder and more and more frequently to get your message across. If you start hitting, where do you stop?*
- *It is sometimes the start of a slippery slope towards harder hitting and even abuse.*
- *It can make children feel hurt, resentful and angry, and may affect the bond between parent and child.*
- *It's undignified and embarrassing for them.*
- *It doesn't show them respect: you wouldn't hit another adult, would you?*
- *They may come to fear, rather than respect, you as a parent.*
- *Children may learn to avoid being smacked by lying or repressing feelings.*

Pulling, pushing, grabbing and gripping

So, in an ideal world, smacking's not a great idea. And, of course, there are other more subtle ways of getting physical which ought really to be avoided, too: sometimes very angry parents – even ones who are very much opposed to smacking – may find themselves gripping a child by the shoulders, roughly grabbing their limbs, or pushing or pulling them in the direction they need them to go in. None of these things is ideal. But they do happen – and almost always when there is some kind of backdrop to that reaction, such as underlying stress.

"It's very normal," reassures Nancy Samalin. "You grip their arm a little too hard or you pull them along and you know you're using force because you're just so helpless. It doesn't mean you're a rotten parent. It just means you had a tough moment that you didn't handle ideally."

I'm not going to say here that you absolutely *mustn't* do these things. (I'd be in no position to – I've been there myself.) Just that you should always strive not to. And the simplest way to do that is to pre-empt those little physical urges before they've had a chance to escape.

When 'time out' matters most

If you feel you're about to get physical, then it's time to pull back sharply. The best thing to do in this situation is to remove yourself from it altogether. Walk away. Take a few moments to feel calm again. More than in any other situation, that all-important pause for thought, or a spot of adult 'time out', is most important if you feel you might actually lash out physically. In these instances, it's *probably* better to do almost anything else that comes to mind than to actually hit them.

"Sometimes, if you can just stop yourself from doing the first thing that you feel, you're going in the right direction," says Nancy Samalin. "What's OK? Overeating, getting in the bath, swearing in the bathroom, throwing plates – though obviously it's better if they're melamine. Anything that will give you a bit of relief but won't harm the child you're mad at."

If it's any consolation, even the experts feel like throttling their kids sometimes. As parenting coach Sue Atkins recalls: "I've been there with my daughter. There was one incident recently when I was busy, I was stressed, they were mucking around, and then when I went up and saw how messy her room was, I went *mad*! I remember thinking it's a good job she's not in the room at the moment because I feel like I could just wallop her around the leg. I was so incandescent I frightened myself. So I went downstairs, burst into tears, had a cup of coffee and told myself to get some perspective!"

Sibling wars

If there's one thing that can really prompt a parent to feelings of violence, it's warring siblings. The fact that it's very normal for siblings to fight isn't always much consolation. Most experts advise us to leave them to it, as far as possible. So the old Time Out for Grown-ups technique is perfectly legitimate here. On the other hand, if they are actually coming to blows or seem likely to, you need to be referee, and if you're going to do that safely, you need to be calm yourself.

"If someone is at risk of harm then, yes, you will probably have to intervene physically, but this doesn't mean getting right in there and joining the boxing match. Ideally you'll do it in a way that's assertive yet not aggressive," says Dr Angharard Rudkin.

So, rather than wading in with the aim of banging their heads together, take that all-important moment to gather strength. Breathe deeply, count to 10, think good thoughts. And remind yourself that screaming and shouting won't calm them, it will probably make them worse. Then you can put your body or an arm in between them, or a firm hand on each of them, perhaps on the chest, and say something short and firm, like: "Stop. Now." Then ask them to go to separate seats or rooms for a moment while they calm down. And make yourself a nice cup of tea.

Always be vigilant for the signs that sibling conflict is brewing and launch in like an Exocet missile with a distraction of some kind – pre-empting violent outbreaks, and therefore your own angry reaction, is always going to be your best chance of dealing with them safely.

> Parents who wish to have a positive impact on sibling skirmishes will want to look for ways to apply the principle of 'less is more'. That is, to let the kids work it out by themselves whenever possible.
> **Gary D. McKay and Steven A. Maybell, from *Calming the Family Storm* (Impact, 2004)**

> The last time I really lost my temper with my kids was whilst driving to a castle during the summer holidays. They were all fighting in the back and it was just me in the front trying to find the way and all I could hear was them screaming and crying. I think it was arguing over some toy that both the boys wanted. This is terrible but I turned round and was trying to get them off each other, whilst driving. My voice was hoarse from shouting and I very nearly stopped the car to try and calm it all down. Sometimes I try and let it ride over me but there comes a point where the noise is so much you just have to control it.
> **Elizabeth, mum to kids aged seven, four and two**

It doesn't happen so much now, but my two have fought a lot, often physically. The main thing about the fighting is to stop it. Sometimes that might mean waiting until they have blown themselves out, then sending them each to their room, which would give me time to think about what to do next, or to talk it over with my husband if he is around. The last time it happened, when they started squabbling over the washing up, we didn't bother sanctioning them afterwards. They'd both got hurt, they were both to blame, and both knew that they'd gone over the top.

When dealing with kids that are fighting you really have to keep hold of your own temper. Rise above it somehow. Easy to say, I know, and not so easy to do. Just try to focus on the bigger picture I guess. And ask yourself 'who is the adult here?'
Emma, mum to kids aged 17 and 14

The last time I lost my rag was over my girls bickering over the most pathetic thing. I yelled, shouted, sent them to their room then regretted it – the yelling and shouting that is. I hate bickering, and that's the thing that's most likely to make me lose it with them.
Alison, mum to kids aged seven, five and two

The eldest tends to whinge about things, such as asking for sweets or some new toy that he wants. He and his sister are always competing over everything: even who gets to be first in the car can be a flashpoint. He cannot stand losing to her, and she's quick to burst into tears if she feels she's been treated unfairly. It's rather like being the referee in a cup final every day.
Tim, dad to children aged five, three and seven months

Hit the pillow, not the kid

For some people, a physical release of anger is a great help. Always best to aim for an inanimate object rather than your child, though. And preferably a soft one, if you don't want to end up with bleeding knuckles, and for obvious household maintenance reasons.

What to do instead

There are plenty of alternatives to smacking. I don't go into them here because this is not a book about dealing with our children's behaviour, it's about dealing with our own responses to it. But of course, there are gazillions of good parenting titles on the shelves that offer lots of advice on the theme. [*Some are recommended on the White Ladder Press website.*]

If you really lose control on a regular basis, or sometimes hurt your children, or frequently come close to hurting them, you may need more help than we can offer here. You should contact an organisation such as Cry-sis, the NSPCC or Parentline Plus (they all have helplines, which are listed on the WLP website), or seek support from a health visitor, GP or social worker.

PARENTS' PANEL: Do you ever get (or have you ever got) physical?

I get most impatient when my daughter is openly defiant or cheeky to me. I've grabbed her arm to march her somewhere and smacked her on her leg or arm on a couple of occasions when I've been really frustrated with her. Usually when I'm tempted I find clenching my fists instead helps.
Jane, mum to kids aged four and five months

I don't believe in smacking children for any reason. However, I did used to 'threaten' my son with smacking him, but he's soon caught on to the fact that I don't ever smack him so I don't even threaten it any more. In my opinion, if you show that smacking is acceptable – for whatever reason – in the home, then you are promoting smacking, hitting or violence outside the home. I did 'squeeze' my son's arm too hard one day – when I was just completely fed up – and it made him cry. I felt so guilty afterwards that I said sorry to him. I haven't done it since.
Maria, mum to a son aged four

No, never smacked, but have wanted to. I shout when I feel that way. If I shout he knows that's it, he has crossed the boundary.
Lynn, mum to boys aged 22, 20, and 13

Yes, I smack sometimes but only because I'm sure it will mean that I won't have to smack as they get older (of course, that's when smacking has no effect and you can't run fast enough to catch them anyway), and so they know my threats aren't empty. I've never 'lost my temper' so to speak when smacking them; it's always been 'controlled'. Although I know there are people who'd say, 'How can any smacking be controlled?'
Fiona, mum to children aged six and four

I never hit my kids. I want to sometimes, but I don't. I do grip very hard or force my three-year-old though when I'm on the edge and he's being obstinate. Yes I sometimes go too far; shouting or gripping and forcing. Time out is good for both of us and I find a cuddle is the cure for almost everything once we're on the same level.
Bill, dad to a son aged three and twins aged 10 months

I've been losing it a little too often lately. I've been poorly and generally tired but still I know in the broad light of day that I should be calmer. I just can't help myself though, when she's continually back-chatting and generally not doing as she's told all the time. It just gets you down.

Last night she refused to go to bed. After repeated calm warnings from me she was still out of bed and was screaming and shouting at me. Eventually I snapped, marched her upstairs, gave her a smack and put her into bed. I hate the fact that I gave her a smack, but sometimes it just seems like the only option left. After that I shut her door and held it closed for a while. Eventually, after we'd both shouted a bit more, she apologised, told me she loved me, and went to bed.

This morning it all started again – she had a hissy fit and threw herself on the floor because I asked her to brush her hair. It just feels like a constant battle at the moment.
Sarah, mum to a daughter aged five

I haven't smacked her yet. That's not to say I won't, and I have come close to it a couple of times and I've found myself using it as a threat. I don't much relish the thought of carrying it through, though, so I really ought to stop that. Recently when I lost my temper I virtually threw her onto the sofa. And I can also remember dragging her by the hand to the naughty step once pretty forcefully.

I don't smack because I'd like to think that I can bring my kids up without having to resort to smacking as a means of disciplining them. My parents used to smack us and I didn't much like it. But then, there's a lot more information and support available to parents nowadays, which there wasn't 30 years ago.
Nina, mum to kids aged four and one

I have reactively smacked my daughter once and remember it clearly. I've never smacked my son. I believe smacking is a response to relieve adult frustration. It doesn't prevent a child from repeating the behaviour – after about 95 percent of

smacks, the child can't remember the behaviour for which they were being smacked.
Simon, dad to kids aged 17 and 14

I have smacked my children in the past, more so when they were smaller. More often than not it was a knee-jerk reaction – they'd run off and I was worried about them, or they would not co-operate and their safety was comprised. And yes, I admit, I smacked sometimes because I had lost my temper or my patience myself. They're too old now. In fact, it would never cross my mind to smack them any more.
Rosie, mum to kids aged 11 and five

I smacked my daughter once on the wrist when she was four and have felt guilty about it ever since. It was my issue, I was tired and frustrated, not hers.
Emma, mum to kids aged 17 and 15

There was one incident when we were shopping and, having threatened to put him in the trolley if he misbehaved, I had to force him in. I did feel really guilty when I bathed him that night and noticed the bruises on his legs where he'd braced himself. Although it was a horrible experience I think I did the right thing by sticking to my guns and carrying out the threat. No one commented and although I felt like everyone was looking at me, no one actually was.

I haven't smacked him – but have come close. There are times when I can *totally* understand why some people are pushed over the edge and hit their children. But I've always managed to draw the line, just.
Claire, mum to a son aged three

I've only smacked him once, when he punched me in the eye, and I just automatically lashed out and caught him with my hand. It's the only time he's ever hit anyone that I am aware of and he's certainly never hit me again. We were both so shocked that we were shaking, and I just walked out of the room and sat on the floor – I was too shaken even to cry. When I went back in, he ran over to me and hugged me and we were both saying "sorry" over and over. I hope I would never do it again.

It's never actually crossed my mind to smack to discipline. I just ignore and walk off, as it works for me.
Jen, mum to boys aged three and nine months

Yes, I've smacked my kids a few times in their lives, although found it to be a useful threat more often. Sometimes I've just found there needs to be *some* resource beyond talking, time out, restriction of privileges, and other similar punishments. I was smacked occasionally as a small child when I'd wilfully done something really naughty, and I remember it as a clear message that I had stepped over a line of acceptable behaviour. So I decided to use smacking as a 'last resort' technique with my children. But I've also used it without warning to the kids, about four times in total, when I wanted to give one of them a big fright if I spotted them doing something that was dangerous and forbidden – perhaps about to start fiddling with an electric plug – and smacked their hand hard and fast out of nowhere. In terms of gripping, forcing, etc, yes, I've done that with both children on a few occasions when I've been absolutely furious with them for some reason, and it hasn't been an appropriate place/time to stop and have a full-scale conversation about the hows, whys and wherefores of the fact their behaviour is not going to be tolerated. But I'm afraid I just don't feel guilty about it.
Deb, mum to kids aged 14 and six

I prefer not to smack my children. It's not a good example for them and merely demonstrates that power wins. I have smacked them when I've reached the end of my tether, and I'm ashamed

of it. I think that to use smacking as a planned strategy is abhorrent and unnecessary. To smack at the end of your tether is understandable, but still an admission of failure and loss of control.
Lucy, mum to boys aged 10 and seven

The couple of times I've ever smacked them made me feel so bad that I didn't try it again. Naughty step, taking away privileges, hugging them so they can't move and then tickling or saying "whatever you do don't laugh" are all more useful. A verse of 'Nobody Loves Me' (which my mum used to sing to me) usually seems to lighten the mood.
Aidan, dad to kids aged 11, five and four

Yes, I do and have smacked, and I would always support a parent using this sparingly if needed. I would always prefer to use other means, but my two-year-old gets a smacked hand for persistently and intentionally stabbing the table with his fork, which is what he did yesterday.
Alison, mum to kids aged seven, five and two

In all honesty, I have smacked them, on the back of the hand. This is only ever done as a last resort when their behaviour is totally out of hand – I hate smacking children and hate to see other people doing it. The most recent smack was issued because one of them deliberately wrecked their siblings' belongings (in a temper) and refused to apologise for doing so. They refused to go to their room and proceeded to call me a bad name. From past experience, I knew that the situation was going to get out of hand (flying ornaments, broken CDs and ripped books) so the only way to end it there and then was to smack on the back of the hand. My children know that a smack is a last resort and that for me to do it means that I am very, very angry with them and they have crossed beyond the point where normal punishment can be used. Thankfully this sort of punishment is used very

rarely. Usually the threat of a smack stops the bad behaviour immediately.
Christine, mum to kids aged 13, 10 and nine

I very rarely smack. The effect is devastating for both parties but incredibly effective, perhaps because it happens so rarely?
Paul, dad to a son aged two

I smacked her once on the hand and it wasn't an appropriate response to what she'd done. In fact I can't even remember what she did. I did it because I'd lost control of the situation and afterwards I realised that. I was really upset by it for weeks and felt really guilty. Since then I've learnt to use other ways of dealing with her behaviour so I don't get to that flashpoint in the first place. It's especially important as I'm constantly tired and don't have the patience I should have as a result. If I ever do get to that point, I will use anything to distract her long enough for me to calm down – TV, toys, reading together, or pushing her around in her toy car.
Pippa, mum to a daughter aged two

We were attempting to get all the kids out of the house in time to get to school when the phone rang and my wife picked up. She was upstairs engrossed in the call while I was trying to persuade our eldest to come downstairs and have her hair brushed whilst also attempting to get the middle one to put her shoes on and the youngest to sit in the buggy. I was getting increasingly fed up at trying to cope alone with all this, and when my daughter rudely said she would not let me brush her hair I just grabbed her and stuck the brush into her tangles and dragged it through, pulling out bits of hair. The end result was that she was weeping in pain, my wife got cross, and I just felt furious with everyone – and guilty, too.
Steve, dad to kids aged eight, six and three

I don't smack them, though once when I was seven months pregnant with the youngest, and the eldest was two, I was feeling really ill one day. He was mucking about as he didn't want to have his nappy changed and we had to go upstairs to do it. I had to haul him upstairs by picking him up which was tough as I was so big by then and feeling ill, and I swore rather nastily in his ear as I carried him up. Then when we got downstairs I put him down very roughly on his feet and pushed him so he fell over and cried. The guilt still lives on – though of course he doesn't remember it.
Moira, mum to kids aged seven, four and two

ANGER MANAGEMENT: top tips from experts

Number six: The Friend Technique

Stop. Think. Try asking yourself how your calmer, wiser friend would react in a situation.

From '*Overcoming Anger and Irritability*', by William Davies (Constable and Robinson, 2000)

PS If you're short on calm and wise friends, you could try calling upon the example of the cool, calm role model of your preference. What would Ghandi have said, for example? How would Jesus have reacted here? Or, Yoda … heeeeelp . . !

7

Happy endings

> Kids learn far better about anger from a parent who is moderately expressive, than one who is always sweet, reasonable, and contained. Kids need to see that parents are human too.
> **Steve Biddulph, from *The Complete Secrets of Happy Children* (Thorsons, 1984)**

Moving swiftly on

Patching things up and moving on after angry outbursts is fundamental to making them matter less – and if you can do so, it's a great life lesson to be passing on. Unless faced with persistently harsh parenting, children are naturally very forgiving and don't tend to bear grudges, but they need a sign from the grown-up they've fallen out with that everything's OK. In any case, it's not emotionally healthy to sulk, hold a grudge, feel vengeful, wallow in guilt or habitually deny you were wrong. And if you have tendencies towards these things, your kids will probably grow up to have them, too.

> A simple apology can diminish resentment and pave the way for reconciliation. Some people are afraid to let their children see that they are vulnerable. But it is a good lesson for children to learn. We are all weak sometimes. And we all have regrets.
> **Nancy Samalin, from *Love and Anger: The Parental Dilemma***

Sorry seems to be ...

Apologies are all-important when you've blown your top in a big way. Saying "sorry" can be cathartic for the person who's lost it, and reassuring for whoever was caught in the firing line. It also helps to draw a line under what's been and gone, clear the air, and return the atmosphere back to a happy one.

"We all lose it sometimes, we're all going to get it wrong, and one way to help restore calm is to say 'sorry' if you've shouted or smacked," says Annette Mountford of Family Links.

Of course, if you were angry in the first place because a child has done something unacceptable, you don't have to let it slide just because you blew your top and you feel bad about it. Carry on with whatever consequences you deem appropriate – but if you know your reaction was OTT all the same, you'll be a bigger person if you can still apologise for it.

"A parent shouldn't grovel just because they feel guilty, and should always make it clear that what the child did wasn't OK. But it's important to acknowledge their own behaviour wasn't OK, either," says Annette.

Don't forget, an apology doesn't have to be "I'm sorry". You could say, "I didn't mean to say that," or "let's make up," if that's any easier.

Don't linger a long while before making amends, if you can help it. Patch things up as soon as possible. And always the same day – don't sleep on it.

> When things go wrong I'll try to reconnect, apologise, and do anything I can to get the show on the road again. I once read that children are like tape recorders – at night they press rewind and relive the events of that day – and I think about that if I ever say anything I regret to them.
> **Sharrone, mum to kids aged four, two and three months**

> I've said horrible things to my daughter and then felt awful. I'll have a cuddle with her, apologise and try to explain why it happened. We've also talked about the concept of grown-ups making mistakes. I think it's important that they know we are not perfect, and I don't feel the need to pretend I am.
> **Charlotte, mum to a daughter aged four and a son aged two**

I didn't mean it

Always take back anything you said that was untrue or frightening for them. And be honest. Let them know why you lost it. If it was something they did that sparked it, then be clear about what it was and quite why it got to you. For example, "I shouted because I felt really frustrated when I wanted you to tidy your room up and you just weren't listening to me."

It's important that children understand any consequences their action or behaviour has prompted – including the way it's made their parents feel. Not only that, but talking through *your* feelings will help them to develop good 'emotional literacy' – a vital range of life skills that include the understanding and management of emotions, and the all-important ability to empathise. And who knows, it may even make them more likely to tidy their room or listen to you next time.

If there were other implicit factors at play – if you were tired, worried, or stressed out about something else, for instance, then it's good to tell them so. Even young children can show surprising levels of understanding and empathy if you let them know you need it (although don't bank on it!). You don't have to give them all the details if it's something that will simply worry them, but you could say something that broadly explains things. For example: "I'm tired and a bit stressed out at the moment. I need you to be good for me."

Don't forget to listen to them at this point, too. Between you, you may be able to come to an agreement that will lessen the chances of a repeat performance.

> As a parent there are times to say, "sorry, I was wrong". How else could I teach them forgiveness?
> **Mike, dad to kids aged 11, nine and six and one month**

Hugs 'n' kisses

A bit of physical contact is a good way to help smooth things over and helps to reassure a child that your love remains unconditional, whatever's just happened. Don't smother them, or force it on them if it's unwanted – wait a while if it seems that a little space is what's needed.

Older kids in particular might not be so keen for a sloppy kiss or a tight embrace. They might well appreciate a more subtle display of physical affection though – a squeeze of the hand, perhaps – which can have just as much impact as big ones.

Ditch the guilt

Apart from anything else, feeling guilty about the way we've treated our children is pointless – what's done is done. In large quantities, guilt is a terrible emotion which can seriously damage a person's happiness and self-esteem.

Don't waste time feeling terrible about it if you went into meltdown and didn't mean it. We're all of us only human. We can only do our best – in life and in parenting. And we all go off the scale sometimes. As Annette Mountford puts it: "We all have bad days, bad months, and even bad years. So yes, you have to forgive yourself. None of us is perfect."

Just to stress that point, here's Nancy Samalin on the subject:

"Most guilt is unproductive. The only advantage to guilt is if you do something really hurtful and it makes you decide not to do it again. So, if you feel guilty for something – telling them you wish they'd never been born, for example – I think it's good if it stops you from saying that again. That's a useful piece of guilt. But if you're constantly apologising and doing the same thing over and over again anyway, then it's useless," she says.

Parenting coach Sue Atkins agrees. "When I've lost my temper with my kids I apologise, of course, because I'm an adult and also because it teaches them it's only right to say sorry when you make a mistake," she says. "I'm a great believer in being honest and open with kids, whatever their age. I think it's OK to say to them, 'look, I've had a bad day', if that's what the problem is.

"So yes, of course we should apologise to our kids. But, as ever, balance is needed. Don't be so apologetic that it could eventually affect your own self-esteem.

"And when you do lose your temper, don't beat yourself up about it. It's like being on a diet and finding yourself scoffing a cream cake one day – there's no point feeling guilty and then giving up. You just start again the next day. Forgive yourself and move forward. And keep trying."

So, if you want to make guilt work for you in a positive way, make a vow to yourself next time you feel guilty about the way that you handled a situation to handle it a bit better next time.

"Having licked our wounds, perhaps we should then seek out ways to help us replace the less stressful times with happier times," suggests Annette Mountford, whose organisation, Family Links, aims to do just that through its courses, and in its book, *The Parenting Puzzle*. There's more information about both on the White Ladder Press website [*details at the end of the book*].

I do usually feel quite guilty after losing my temper, and sometimes ask myself how I could have handled it differently. But then I console myself by thinking that life is never going to be 100 percent perfect for them, and they need to learn that their irritating behaviour has consequences.
Juliet, mum to three kids aged eight, six and three

My husband was away and I was home alone with my daughter, having had an exhausting week. She was playing a little with her food, so I retreated to the kitchen to load the dishwasher – I have a thing about food mess. I came in with dessert, completely unprepared for the redecorating job done in my absence. Food was absolutely everywhere – in her hair, down her front, up the walls, over the table and floor, on the curtains, and still on her plate. She'd barely eaten a thing. I carried her upstairs to clean her, where she proceeded to hit me for moving her, and covered me in food too.

That was it, I lost it and shouted at her. I couldn't help myself. I was tired and teary and cross with myself for letting it get to me. I looked her in the eye and told her how upset I was about the mess and about being hurt. She continued to hit me, so instead of being calm I got louder. As soon as I had lost it I regretted it, and apologised immediately.

I spent all night patiently waiting for her to cry so I could rush in and show her what a good mother I could be really. But she slept through the night. Despite my guilt, she hugged and kissed me as usual and didn't seem at all fazed by my behaviour.
Sonia, mum to a daughter aged 16 months

Analyse that

Although it's pointless to ruminate endlessly (and negatively) about a situation, and it's important not to feel guilty about it, it's also worth taking a moment to work out what went wrong and why. This is especially important if losing your temper is becoming a regular thing, or the same old flashpoints keep recurring and causing the same old rows. Briefly replay the scenario in your mind and think about how you ended up there and how you might avoid it the next time.

If your stress levels are high generally or there's something running a little deeper which prompted you to feel angry in the first place – perhaps because of what's going on at work, money worries, or problems in another relationship – aim to tackle it outside of your dealings with the kids. It's not really fair to displace your adult worries and let them affect how you treat your children.

Don't dwell on it

Let teenagers have the monopoly on the incredible sulks. There is nothing to be gained by dwelling on a situation that's made you cross or to hold it against a person for longer than necessary.

Encourage them to do the same by drawing a veil over the situation and moving on to something else, together if possible. If you still feel sore and you're really not up for a jolly, redemptive game of rounders, let them get on with their own thing for a while and retreat elsewhere for some calming down time on your own. But be sure to make friends first.

Put your anger into action

At the beginning of the book I said that anger could sometimes be positive because it can help people act on a situation that's making them cross. That can work in families, too – an angry parent can be an inspired one. For instance, if no one's helping with the housework, you could set about drawing up a rota and calling a family meeting to thrash the matter out. If you have issues with getting dressed in the morning, crank up some kind of system – a reward chart, perhaps, or an agreement to select and lay out clothes the night before – that will help make it less of a problem.

Reward yourself when you *do* get it right

Spend a few moments mentally patting yourself on the back every time you deal with a difficult situation in a cool, calm manner. Or reward yourself in a more tangible way.

(Oops, there we go with the chocolate and wine again ...)

> If you have decided to respond (not react) to today's anger in a different way than you have in the past, feel good about yourself. There is nothing like the feeling of being in charge of your emotions.
> **W. Doyle Gentry, from *Anger Management for Dummies* (Wiley 2007)**

PARENTS' PANEL: Do you ever feel bad – and what do you do to make things better?

I have in the past become too angry. I shout very loudly. Always regret it, always apologise profusely and always try not to do it again. (It has reduced considerably!)
Simon, dad to kids aged 17 and 14

Yes, I feel guilty about my selfishness and crabbiness, on average I guess about three times every day.
Deb, mum to kids aged 14 and six

Sometimes you can forget they're only very young. I got really angry with my daughter a while back – I can't for the life of me

remember why right now – but she went to her room and I went up five minutes later and apologised to her. My mistake is that I find it hard to 'let go' of the thing they've done if it was particularly naughty. I tend to forget that with young children, one telling-off at the time is generally sufficient. I'm sure they feel bad enough without me labouring the point.
Fiona, mum to kids aged six and four

It was supper time for our twins who were both tired and ravenous, which meant the only thing they were able to concentrate on was screaming their heads off, in stereo. Feeding them then became a test of will and nerve, which I quickly lost. I grabbed one of them (the loudest) – probably too roughly and put him in the bathroom, shut the door and went back to the other. I made myself a coffee and drank it, staring coldly at her whilst she continued screaming (strangely she was unperturbed by my cold stare). Then having told myself several times 'I'm the grown up here', I fed her, mildly improving her mood. I put her in front of the television and went to get the other one, who was still beside himself. I fed him, by now shaking and sweating. Finally it dawned on me that the way to calm all of us down was to put them in the bath, which has an instant effect on their mood. They cheered up immediately – I washed my face and tried to assuage my guilt by apologising to my son, who by the looks of things wasn't in the least bit concerned, so long as he could chew a bath toy.
Bill, dad to a son aged four and twins aged 10 months

I always regret shouting. I went through a phase when my shouting was bad, so I asked the girls to make me a star chart, and I got a star if I'd managed not to shout for a day.
Alison, mum to kids aged seven, five and two

I always feel guilty after I've lost my temper and shouted at them. We normally 'make up' afterwards and sit down for

cuddles which helps ease the guilt. I feel more useless than anything – because I couldn't control them and it got to the point of me screaming blue murder at them.
Sharron, mum to girls aged six, three, and six months

My daughter was being generally whingy and annoying and then started demanding things. She'd already been rude to my mother and I cannot abide rudeness. I grabbed her arm and dragged her upstairs, throwing her into her room and shutting the door. After a while we both calmed down and had a cuddle. I had to remember that the day before had been one of those milestone days: first ever recorder lesson followed by first ever tap and modern class followed by lots of enthusiasm and recorder practice. She must have been exhausted – she is only five.
Helen, mum to kids aged five and two

I really lost it recently and as always I transformed from a relatively well-mannered woman into the psycho bitch from hell with the voice of a fishwife. Afterwards tears were shed, apologies and promises made (all round), followed by guilty hugs and cuddles. I believe very strongly in the 'never go to bed on an unresolved argument' theory. As to how this made me feel – like a huge failure, with a big dollop of guilt thrown in. I know you're not meant to shout at your children, I know you're not meant to have unrealistic expectations, but I am only human, and sometimes, just sometimes, what you're meant to do doesn't quite have the desired effect. Needless to say my boys were the epitome of loveliness afterwards – for about 24 hours.
Helen, mum to sons aged 10 and seven

Occasionally, yes I do feel guilty, and I try and apologise to them but still let them know that what they did was wrong and that I am apologising for over-reacting. I'm sure they've got the odd extra 'treat' as a result though.
Andy, dad to daughters aged six and three

We make sure we always make up before bedtime – the old adage 'never let the sun go down on your anger' is core for us.
Steve, dad to kids aged seven, five and two

Talking through events later when things are calm has a very positive effect, but you have to be honest and say what you did wrong and how you felt.
Aidan, dad to kids aged 11, five, and four

I think it is very important to be able to say sorry to your kids if you've made a mistake, gone over the top, or whatever. You need to show that nobody is above making a mistake – people who advocate never admitting a weakness to their kids are just wrong. Kids need to know what's happening, so we always explain why decisions are made. They may not like it, nor agree, but that's just tough.
Emma, mum to kids aged 17 and 14

All my children know I have a long fuse. It's too long and probably lulls them into a false sense of security. I'm just made that way. However, my shout carries a Government health warning – if you've been on the receiving end then you've had it coming for ages, which is why I rarely feel guilty about using it. To conclude a 'shout-off', the offending child will be asked by my wife to apologise for causing me to get out the big guns, to which I will usually give them a kiss and say, "Well done for saying sorry. Now take the staples out of your sister."
Nick, dad to kids aged, 16, 14 and five and twins of 11.

My son was hungry and cross (admittedly my fault, I'd got caught up in a hectic day at work and started tea too late) and once I'd finally got food on the table he threw his bowl of pasta on the floor in a huff. I calmly picked it up and salvaged what I could of the pasta, but the same thing happened again. So I quickly rustled up some houmous on toast instead. That, too, went on the floor. Again, I picked it up, put it on his plate, and again it was chucked on the floor. Until then, I'd been calm and had ignored him, hoping he'd get bored with acting up, but at that point I snapped. I turned to him and yelled: "That's enough! You're really pissing me off now! Stop throwing your food on the bloody floor!" He must have sensed the fury in my voice because he very quietly ate all his toast, asked for more, meekly requested a yoghurt and ate the lot without another squeak. Afterwards, I didn't feel guilty – I felt great. OK, I could have chosen better, more constructive language, but I've only ever shouted at him once or twice before and maybe, because of that, it meant I could regain control of the situation. I needed him to know there was a limit to my patience. When he got down from the table, we had a cuddle and did a drawing together, so I think we sort of made up. Afterwards I wondered if I could have done things differently – maybe I should have cleared the food away and let him get down from the table, sending him to bed on an empty stomach, rather than shouting. But then that's the lot of being a mum – the endless guilt and should-haves.

Hannah, mum to a son aged 16 months

ANGER MANAGEMENT: top tips from experts

Number seven: The Lifesavers Technique*

Suck on a boiled sweet. This technique takes advantage of the link between the sucking reflex and achieving a state of calm that's evident in all newborn infants. It involves the ingestion of something sweet, as sweet sensations are associated at the level of the brain with pleasure, which is the antithesis of anger.** It also buys you enough time to formulate a response to your initial anger instead of just reacting to it. And not only that, but if you've something in your mouth, you can't verbalise your anger in ways that escalate the conflict or cause you regret later on.

From *Anger Management for Dummies* by W. Doyle Gentry (Wiley, 2007)

*America has a brand of sweets called Livesavers, hence this technique's name. We Brits could perhaps rename it the Murray Mint Technique.

**So you see, there *is* a good reason why you should eat chocolate when you feel angry ...

8

How to have a cooler, calmer lifestyle

Lady:	Listen, it seems to me you have some anger management issues.
Lynette:	I have four children under five. I absolutely have anger management issues.

from *Desperate Housewives*

Be cool

We've talked a lot about what happens in the heat of the moment. But how about more generally? It stands to reason that a person who has a cooler, calmer attitude to life in general is going to cope better than someone who's habitually stressed out when faced with hassles at home. There are all sorts of ways you might look at doing this. Here are a few ideas to get you started.

Practise positive parenting

It may sound a bit touchy-feely, but positive parenting is a philosophy that's championed by most of the experts these days.

The basic theory is that the more positive you are when things are going well, the less likely they are to go wrong in the future. It requires quite a bit of conscious effort to make it a permanent habit, but it does start to come more naturally the more you try.

And there's no doubt that when it's working, there are rosy glows all round.

"If you parent positively your children feel good about themselves, and you feel good about yourself," says Annette Mountford of Family Links, which runs courses specifically aimed at spreading the positive parenting message.

Here's what positive parenting is all about, according to the NSPCC:

- *Showing your kids loads of unconditional love and affection, all the time.*
- *Praising them lavishly when they behave well.*
- *Setting a good example with your own behaviour.*
- *Listening to their points of view and encouraging them to find their own resolutions to difficult situations.*
- *Steering clear of harsh punishments – and trying hard not to lose your temper.*
- *Having a clear set of rules, boundaries and limits, so kids know exactly where they stand.*

Stop feeling so guilty!

As we've seen, modern parents suffer a great deal from guilt. We all seem increasingly obsessed with getting our parenting 'right' these days, and inevitably we feel bad when we see ourselves as failing – which is frequently, because it's darn impossible always to be 'right' where parenting is concerned.

But guilt isn't good! It knocks confidence, enhances anxiety, and certainly isn't conducive to cool, calm, parenting. Or indeed a cool, calm life in general.

I'm not going to tell you to stop feeling guilty. Or rather, I *am* going to tell you to stop feeling guilty. I just know perfectly well that you won't, because for most of us, it's ingrained. Nevertheless, please try. Here are a few thoughts to get you going:

- Ignore other people with strong opinions on the way you bring up your children. You know best. It's none of their business.
- Don't compare yourself to other parents. Raising children is not a competitive sport. Anyway, Alpha Mum over there is a silly bitch, and no one likes her.
- Refer to the mass media for sources of parenting advice by all means. But think of it as guidance, not gospel. That way, if it doesn't actually work for you, it won't matter.
- Accept your limitations. Having it all's a myth. There's no such thing as a perfect parent.
- Lower your standards. Cut yourself (and your kids) some slack.
- Do *whatever you need to do* to be a fulfilled and happy individual outside your role as a parent: work, play, relax. And do it with pride.

> There's so much pressure on parents, especially mums, to be perfect in a Nigella Lawson meets Annabel Karmel kind of way. The myth of the yummy mummy has a lot to answer for. You've got to be slim, sexy, in control – and know how to whip up wholemeal muffins for your perfect children without a kitchen catastrophe to boot. It's bollocks, really bollocks.
> **Hannah, mum to a son aged 16 months**
>
> From the minute he was born I've had two imaginary over-bearing women on my left and right shoulders, casting judgement on my parenting skills. One says "you're spoiling that child, he'll end up a sissy and a mummy's boy" and the other says "that poor child, he hardly gets to see much of you and you can't even be bothered to give him your full attention when you do spend time together. He's going to grow up a thug and resent you for ever." Doesn't everyone have that, or is it just me?
> **Alison, mum to a son aged two**

Talk about it (or write about it)

Don't bottle up feelings of anger, frustration and unhappiness. Tell someone you trust – but preferably an adult, as it's not much fun for kids to be burdened with that sort of stuff. If anger or stress is becoming a real issue and life is getting you down, consider seeking some professional support from a health visitor, GP or counsellor.

If you can't talk about it, try writing about it. Many experts espouse the benefits of keeping a journal – as well being a good way to get things off your chest, it can help identify causes and patterns of anger and stress and, therefore, be a good start in tackling them.

Write down all the stressful factors in life or the triggers that make you mad. Then you can go about thinking of ways of eliminating these things from your life – or simply working out ways to stop them mattering so much.

They'll be there for you

Friends – the supportive, non-judgemental kind, of course – are a real boon when you're a parent. Particularly so if you're at home during the day with pre-school children, when the walls around you can sometimes feel like bars, and the company you keep is, frankly, at times lacking.

Non-parent friends are nice to keep, as a reminder that there is life outside your family. But in particular, the support and empathy of other parents is one of the best ways to feel confident in your own parenting. And if you're confident, you're more likely to be calm.

It's usually pretty easy to make pals among other parents – at playgroups, outside the school gates, or just mooching in the park. And once you've met one it will usually lead to many other introductions. If you're struggling to meet anyone in the flesh, try logging on to an online parents' support network such as Netmums [*www.netmums.com*] for advice and friendship.

Count your blessings

When all's said and done, it's great to have kids and to be part of a loving family. Some people aren't so lucky. Without wishing to sound Pollyanna-ish, it's always good to keep that at the forefront of your mind.

> What's wonderful about my kids? The fact that they love me, even though I sometimes make shocking decisions – as a parent and as a human being.
> **Deb, mum to kids aged 14 and six**

Slow down

There are loud calls for the 'slowing down' of childhood – and life in general – at the moment. And hurrah to that. We're all trying to do too much, in too short a time. And stress is catching – if you're constantly on edge, your kids will be too. Children thrive on relaxed, laid-back lifestyles – and so do grown-ups.

Maybe a major downsizing programme and a significant lifestyle change is out of the question for you at the moment. But that's no reason not so seek out smaller ways of slowing down, wherever possible. Worry less about cramming in quality time, organised formal activities and structured weekend timetables, and try just hanging out together – outside, if at all possible, as fresh air and nature can be a real tonic for stressed-out parents and children.

Aim to slow down in your day-to-day business, too. Remember that children have a totally different concept of time to ours. They don't really grasp deadlines and schedules the same way – and bloody good luck to them. So always allow twice as long to get anything done. And try to ask yourself: 'Do I actually need to be in this place, at this time?' You might well find you're rushing unnecessarily. Take life at a child's pace whenever possible. In other words: if you can dawdle, do.

> I think the key to being a happier parent is to get more sleep and to have less stress at work, and more time at home, doing things with your kids. That's the general lifestyle in New Zealand, where we're currently living. I've genuinely noticed a huge change in my relationship with the kids since we've been here – for the better.
> **Simon, dad to kids aged 17 and 14**
>
> I find going to the park regularly a great release. I chuck him in the pushchair and then we run around like loons in the grass and both let off steam.
> **Hannah, mum to a son aged 16 months**

Get a good night's sleep

Being a parent is an exhausting business. However, a full night's sleep can elude you for many years after you become one. But the fact is, we all need to sleep at night to help us get through the day. Just as small children get grumpy, irrational and irritable when they are tired, so do grown-ups.

There are actually very few reasons why you *shouldn't* be able to get a full night's sleep once a child is past six months. There are plenty of good books and websites where you can get solid advice on how to achieve this – and if you're really desperate, there are both private and NHS sleep clinics that can help you out. There are more details about both of these things on the White Ladder Press website.

According to the experts, the key to a good night's sleep is an appropriate bedtime and a consistent, calming routine beforehand, for children of all ages. The other massive advantage to this kind of set-up is that it allows you to have child-free evenings which, for a lot of parents, is essential to their relaxation at the end of the day. And even if your children are too old for a nice early bedtime, you can still insist on the evenings being for 'quiet time', perhaps spent in their bedrooms.

Of course, many families prefer to spend this time together and if that's what constitutes a cool, calm ending to the day round at your house, you should carry on.

Eat well

Don't forget to eat. Like children, adults need to feed their bodies to have healthy minds, and low energy levels can lead to short fuses. Sometimes, as with small people, all it takes is a well-timed banana to improve your mood. Aim to eat healthily, too, as a nutrient-rich diet helps to combat stress.

Look after your love life

You can't be a cool, calm person if you don't have adequate support from your partner. And if there are difficulties in your relationship, there's every chance that you'll transfer them to your children – even if you don't mean to – so you owe it your kids to sort them out. Relate would be a good place to start: they're listed in all local phone books.

Even if things are fine and dandy between you, don't let your love life slide. Squeeze in some 'you 'n' me' time whenever you can – even if you can't find or afford a babysitter, make a date in your own dining room. And keep talking. Communication really counts in families.

Take time out from parenting

Every parent deserves a bit of time to pursue an interest, paint their toenails, spend time with their own grown-up friends, and just generally be a human being in their own right rather than someone's mum or dad. Make sure you get yours when it's due.

If you're divorced or separated and your children spend time with your ex, make the most of the time without them. And if you're a lone parent without much in the way of support or babysitting services, make it an aim to get some – offer to swap favours with a friend, if need be.

> When it gets really bad I resent being on my own and having to deal with it all, but I get on with it. And, hard as it can be sometimes not having someone to hand over to when the going gets tough, I can look forward to some real 'me' time when she's with her dad for the weekend.
> **Sarah, mum to a daughter aged five**
>
> Luckily their grandparents are obliging enough for me to have the odd day out every so often with my hubby. And as they're at full-time school, I get a break then and go to the gym. I must admit that having them in their rooms from about 7.30pm on a school night enables me (and them) to relax.
> **Rosie, mum to boys aged 11 and five**
>
> My lifesaver was sending him to a day nursery when he was two for two mornings a week. It just let me get my head straight, go to the gym, get some work done and generally feel like me again for a few hours a week.
> **Claire, mum to a son aged three**
>
> Having time away from the kids is vital. For me this comes from going to work and Sunday mornings alone at church. If getting away from the kids is not an option then a change of environ-

ment such as going to the park or taking them for a walk in the country is a good way to release the tensions.
Tim, dad to kids aged five, three and seven months

Get some exercise (or at least some relaxation)

Stop groaning at the back – it's a medical fact: regular exercise really does relieve stress and helps aid sleep. Admittedly, a hard hour's work-out can seem like the last thing on your mind after a day at the coalface of parenting, at work, or some combination of both. But make the effort, and you'll be glad you did.

If you can't find the time or inclination to exercise, then at least make time to relax. You don't have to put on a leotard, contort yourself into a strange shape and meditate for two hours – just take 10 minutes a day to practise some deep-breathing techniques and some gentle stretches.

Introduce a sport or activity into your lifestyle as a family, and you'll be killing two birds with one stone – keeping fit *and* hanging out together.

PARENTS' PANEL: What do you do to be a cooler, calmer, person?

Sleep usually works for me – I blame any crabbiness on my part on a lack of it (and a bit on running my own business). I also go running. And talking to my patient, loving, caring, infinitely-better-than-me-at-calming-a-situation-down husband. And, of course, sharing a glass of vino with him after they've gone to bed.
Fiona, mum to kids aged six and three

It's a cliché, but having some me-time always helps as it helps me

to remember that I'm still me, not just a stay-at-home-mother. Letting off steam talking to friends is a lifesaver, too.
Jane, mum to kids aged four and five months

Much as we rant and rave most days about something insignificant, we also think at some point during each day that we are so lucky to have two healthy gorgeous boys who have taught us so much about ourselves, each other and life in general. And if we get through this parenting lark with our minds and bodies intact and are lucky enough to enjoy the adults that they will become, then that has to be our greatest achievement. (Of course, if I find myself visiting them in a top security establishment and can only communicate with them through bulletproof glass – that will also be down to me, and the guilt will continue to haunt me.) It really helps to savour the good.
Helen, mum to sons aged 10 and seven

I find that going to the gym has given me a chance to think about myself. It's only for half an hour, maybe three times a week, but it does make a huge difference. I really bash it all out on the machines. Another good thing for me is my book club (seriously). We go out to a restaurant, so that no one has to bother with mess and preparation, and we natter all night long. When the eldest was little, I really loved the time we spent with our baby club. I found it reassuring to know that we were all experiencing the same things and I knew that I wasn't alone.
Angila, mum to kids aged six and two

- Shopping.
- Home study (to take time out and stop my brain turning to mush).
- Copious amounts of Pinot Grigio!

Siobhan, mum to a son aged 17 months

I go for long runs twice a week which I find really relaxing and is good 'head space' which helps me put things into perspective. The boys might have been driving me mad before I went out but after 10 gruelling miles on a Sunday morning it's great to get home to be greeted rapturously by the eldest shouting "Daddy, Daddy" and throwing his arms around me.

We try to get the toys out of the lounge at night so we're not surrounded by their clutter and to give us our space back. Also, we often eat dinner with the boys during the week but Friday and Saturday nights we have a grown-up meal with just the two of us which is great (even if my wife does insist on watching the X Factor afterwards.) And we try to book a babysitter and get out for a proper 'date' once a month.
Adrian, dad to boys aged three and one

Sharing the load helps a lot. For example, taking it in turns to go in if our daughter is having a rough night (we'll both be awake, anyway). Also, trying not to do something else when she's wanting your time – it takes twice as long as attending to her first and then doing whatever it is.

As for relaxation, hmmm, what's that? Distraction therapy works for me. I try to find something totally un-child related to do when I have a few minutes to myself (read a book, nose around on the web, etc).
Sean, dad to a daughter aged one

Joining a gym. Having a partner who'd take over so I could have space and time for myself and was prepared to share night duties equally. Seeing friends with children who had the same highs and lows. Buying a dishwasher. Reading a decent newspaper and listening to Radio 4 when they were asleep. Getting out of the house at least once a day.

And doing good things together as a family – even a quick walk by the sea on a weekend helps one to remember life is good and

having a family is life-enhancing. At 4.30pm on a wet Tuesday it is so easy to forget that.
Lucy, mum to sons aged 10 and seven

I always try to leave enough time to do the things I need to do so it's not stressful for either of us. I know that if I need to go to town, for instance, she'll want to walk so that's going to take 30 minutes instead of the five minutes it would take with the pushchair. So I leave 30 minutes to do it in and we both enjoy ourselves. I apply the same principle to everything and if something isn't urgent I leave it until another day so that I'm never too pressurised.
Pippa, mum to a daughter aged two

Self-hypnosis has been a wonderful tool for me finally to learn how to relax properly and give me time out, even if it's just 10 minutes. Also, we try to set some time aside (little and often and making sure we all stick to it) to really listen to each other, because normally we all just talk at one another with not a lot of listening happening.

And I try to eat the occasional special meal separate from them. Mealtimes can be so unpleasant with teenagers!
Rebecca, mum to daughters aged 16 and 13

I'm rigid about bedtimes. I know that no matter what happens during the day, come 8pm, the youngest two will be in bed and it will be 'my time'. It's a bit like knowing there is a light at the end of the tunnel.
Christine, mum to kids aged 13, 10 and nine

I would say that it's spending time with the kids that helps me cope with the stresses and strains in the rest of my life. It's remarkable how it puts things in perspective – you realise a meeting isn't so important or a deadline so critical.

My wife points out that I do disappear to the gym and to watch football more than I used to, but I think that's because there's a lot less sex, drugs and rock 'n' roll than there used to be before I was a dad. You need something to fill the void!
David, dad to daughters aged nine, five, three and two months

Having a couple of really good friends who you don't mind letting in the house when it's a tip so you can have a good cry, or moan. Especially if they've been through it before you.
Carol, mum to a daughter aged one

For sanity's sake, my husband takes her for a whole day every few weeks so that I can go shopping, go to the hairdressers, just feel normal. He gets wound up too sometimes, so he buggers off to kick boxing and works it out of his system. I'm far too lazy to be that energetic, but doing exercise definitely helps.
Verity, mum to a daughter aged one

I like to disappear to the swimming pool once, maybe twice a week if I can fit it in. Just a half-hour's swimming on my own helps me sort out 'stuff' in my mind. I also prepare tea for the following day the night before, to avoid any stress come 5pm with a houseful of hungry girls. I like cooking in the evening, so it's another chance to wind down.

Come 8pm, the children are told that they no longer exist in my little world (unless they're staying up specially for a Strictly Come Dancing final or we're doing something else special). Packed lunches are done before 8pm, uniforms laid out, and the dishwasher's on, so I'm not doing any housework in the evening and it's definitely grown-up time.
Sharon, mum to daughters aged nine, five, three, and two months

I think the key is being as rested as possible, which I'm only now learning to do. It sounds great in principle but when the only

time you have to yourself is once the kids are in bed then you find yourself trying to squeeze in too much (work you've brought home, cleaning, tidying, essential paperwork, TV watching, listening to music, playing music, hobbies). I've noticed that the way I interact with the kids, ie the amount of patience I've got, is directly affected by how calm and reasonable I'm feeling generally. We need to take time just to recharge, but in 21st century Britain there just ain't the time.
Aidan, dad to kids aged 11, five and four

ANGER MANAGEMENT: top tips from experts

Number eight: The Turtle Technique

Pretend to be protected by a shell, simply not responding to provocation.

From *Anger Management: A Practical Guide*, by Adrian Faupel, Elizabeth Herrick and Peter Sharp (David Fulton, 1998)

The cool, calm conclusion

Well, that's pretty much all the advice I have up my sleeve on how to be a cooler, calmer parent. I hope that if – like me – you're a mum or dad with a short fuse and you would much prefer it to be longer, you'll have found some of these ideas useful and that, in putting them into practice, you're at least a bit cooler and calmer than you used to be.

I aim to take my own advice, each and every day of my life – and I'm a lot happier for it. I still hit the roof sometimes, triggered by moments of extreme stress, or by the irritating tendencies of those offspring of mine. But these days when my kids wave that red rag under my nose, I'm much more inclined to walk away or aim my rage in a direction other than theirs.

I've stopped beating myself up about it, too. There doesn't seem much point. And when all's said and done, my children still seem to love me, strops and all. As one of my parent panellists has already commented: how cool is that?